SKIN DIVERS IN ACTION

Apart from the whales and fishes inhabiting the ocean, today finds a growing number of people beneath the sea — for pleasure, for science, for profit.

In this newest "In Action" book, the authors bring together the science and mystery of diving, from the kind of gear necessary to the wonders of the ocean depths. All the information about the dangers and safety measures of this popular sport is included. Skin diving as it's done by the Navy frogmen, the treasure hunt explorations, and the old art of diving are discussed in detail.

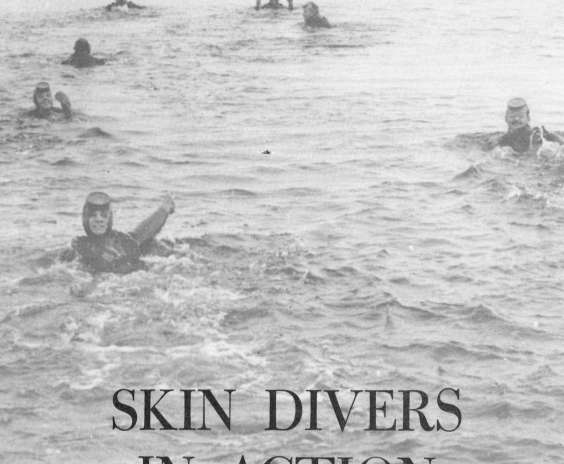

SKIN DIVERS
IN ACTION

By Erik Bergaust and William Foss

G. P. Putnam's Sons   New York

The "Science In Action" Books
by Erik Bergaust and William Foss

HELICOPTERS IN ACTION
COAST GUARD IN ACTION
THE MARINE CORPS IN ACTION
SKIN DIVERS IN ACTION

Fourth Impression

Contents

ACKNOWLEDGMENTS

Skin diving is one of the fastest-growing sports in America. It has also become a profession and, finally, it has created a new breed of soldier — the frogman.

If practiced soundly, diving builds a strong, healthy body. Any good swimmer in good physical condition can become a good diver. But he must know much about the possible dangers and all the tricks of the trade in order to dive safely. In this book, therefore, we have put great emphasis upon the safety aspects and dangers of skin diving. A young diver must understand these elements fully and should make it a point to learn the scientific aspects of diving. Only then will he become a safe and good diver, and only then will he enjoy the wonderful world that is the skin diver's alone.

This book is the product of much research. It could not have been done without assistance rendered by the United States Navy, the U. S. Naval School Deep Sea Divers' Lieutenant Commander Robert Pescott, Lieutenant Victor Evans, and Lieutenant Walter R. Bergman. We wish to thank them for their invaluable assistance. Thanks also to Mike Freeman, who helped provide the information on treasure hunting; to the Conference for National Cooperation in Aquatics for permission to use their official glossary; and to the U. S. Divers Company and American Water Sports Company for the use of their illustrations.

ERIK BERGAUST and WILLIAM FOSS
Washington, D.C.

1

Going into the Water

HAVE you ever wondered about the sea as you watched
the waves break upon the beach in a froth of white
bubbles? Have you wondered about the fish and monsters that
may live within the depths of the ocean and the lakes?

The sea has a geography and a life of its own. There are rivers
in the sea, and these are called currents. The currents are caused
by winds and tides. The rotation of the earth has an effect on the
flow of currents as well. Currents will carry schools of fish long
distances; tropical fish have appeared in the northern hemisphere
because of the action of the currents.

The earth is divided into two hemispheres, the shape and divi-
sion of which can be illustrated by an orange cut directly in
half. Water covers three quarters of the earth's surface. The gravitational force of the moon upon the earth's surface creates tides,

which in turn create currents. The earth is constantly rotating and this rotation also has an effect upon the movement of the water. Currents tend to rotate in a circular direction. Picture a clock and the movement of the hands. The currents in the northern hemisphere move in a clockwise direction, to the right. Currents in the southern hemisphere move in a counterclockwise direction, to the left.

The currents will carry either cold or warm water. The Labrador Current flows off the coast of Newfoundland and Greenland and the icy waters flow into the Atlantic Ocean. The South Equatorial Current flows near the coast of Brazil, bringing its warm waters with it.

One of the two major currents in the northern hemisphere is the Gulf Stream, which flows along the eastern coast of the United States from the waters near Florida. The Gulf Stream is approximately 95 feet wide and almost a mile deep. The other major current is the Japanese Current, which flows in a clockwise direction from the coast of Japan to the coast of California. It will carry the warm waters off the Pacific coast; the water is colder there in the summer than along the Atlantic coast.

It was not known whether undersea currents existed or not until the descent on January 23, 1960, of a deep-sea diving vessel, the bathyscaph *Trieste*, to the bottom of a deep ocean trench near the island of Guam. One of the main purposes of this record-breaking and historic dive was to find out if fish lived at such great depths in the ocean. If they did, that would show the presence of undersea currents that carry oxygen and marine life to great depths. As was stated by Jacques Piccard, the great pioneer who performed this dive, in the August, 1960, issue of *National Geographic Magazine:*

U. S. Navy

The *Trieste* bathyscaph represents what oceanographers and Navy experts think will lead to new underwater technologies, rescue equipment, and ways of underwater searching, salvaging, and hunting — whether it be for gold or scientific information.

We were not, however, the first messengers from the surface. The creatures we had seen verified the long-assumed existence of undersea currents bringing oxygen down to the very bottom of the sea. As yet we do not know the exact speed or size of these currents, but apparently there must be massive exchanges of water between the surface and the great depths.

The diver is not as much concerned with these currents as he is with tidal currents and *backwash*, which is the current that is created when the tides recede. A diver must be aware of the movements of the tide and the geography of the ocean bottom where he dives. An experienced diver can tell a little about the ocean bottom by the breaking of the waves on the shore and the patterns they form.

A wave is composed of a *crest* and a *trough*. The crest is the part of the wave that rises before it breaks upon the shore. The trough is the part in front of it, the lowest point.

Like the land, the water has small mountains, made up of rock, sand, and coral. A coral reef is made up of small organisms, living and dead, called *polyps*. The polyps utilize the calcium in the water to build up hard little shells. Many ships have been wrecked upon coral reefs, and divers have been cut and infected working around them. Coral infection is one of the hazards of diving and must be treated with antibiotics. Swelling of the hands results from this type of infection and the diver often cannot use his hands for periods of up to three weeks.

Reefs of rock, sand, and coral, in warm seas and oceans only, lie at different points near the coasts of the various continents. The reefs of sand are called sandbars. Usually the reefs do not form a solid line, but are broken at various points into chains. The diver must be concerned with the currents that flow in and out of these reefs. They are called *rip currents* and can be identified by the breaking of the waves and the foam that is always found near them. An experienced diver can read the movements of the waves almost as one can read a map. Waves break continuously over a reef. If waves move toward the shore in a continuous unbroken line, the presence of a reef nearby is not likely. Waves will break near small rocks in the ocean as well as large reefs and wave movement is an important study to an experienced diver. A complete knowledge of the movement of the tides and the general geography of the ocean, lake, or river floor where a dive is planned is quite necessary.

A diver can be carried great distances by currents if he is caught, and it is better for him to allow the current to carry him than to fight its force. Exhaustion can easily result, and the diver would be wise to conserve his strength.

Instead of valleys the ocean is filled with great trenches. The trench in which the bathyscaph *Trieste* dived is the deepest in the world; it is almost seven miles deep. The pressure of the water at such a great depth is tremendous and for this reason it was unknown whether any marine life could exist, but it does. These great trenches exist all over the ocean floor and many of them have been unexplored, as until the invention of the bathyscaph exploration of these trenches was not possible.

An astounding amount of marine life populates the waters covering the earth, including the rivers, lakes, and seas. What kind of life is this? What kind of plants live in the ocean?

A diver can become entangled in the masses of exotic plant life; extreme care must be taken by divers to avoid this. The propellers of ships are sometimes caught in masses of kelp and other sea-

The famous oceanographic research vessel *Trieste* being loaded aboard a Navy ship for a special search mission in the Atlantic for the sunken *Thresher* submarine. The *Trieste* is a bathyscaph. It was built in 1953 in Italy.

U. S. Navy

weeds, and the ships cannot move until the plants are either disentangled or cut away. In certain seas great masses of these plants are found, and ships avoid these areas if possible.

The four major oceans are the Atlantic, the Pacific, the Indian, and the Arctic. The remainder of the world's salt waters are broken up into seas and gulfs. By studying a globe one can easily identify the various oceans and seas.

The marine life in the ocean ranges from the tiny one-celled *diatom* to the giant mammal, the whale. Whales are very rarely found in shallow water and many tales have been told of these giants of the sea, such as the story of Moby Dick and others. The whale supplies oil for many purposes — including the making of lipstick!

Plankton, which is only slightly larger than the diatom, feeds upon it. The larger species, including whales and sharks, feed on plankton.

Aside from the whale the largest and most dangerous species of marine life are sharks, barracuda, octopuses, squid, sting rays, electric sting rays, and moray eels.

Some sharks are found only in warm waters and others are found in all oceans. They range in size from 5 to 60 feet. Contrary to legend, sharks are not all dangerous man-eaters. Sharks will attack divers if there is any blood in the area from freshly killed fish or a bleeding wound, or if the diver is mistaken for a fish because of the shark's poor eyesight. There are twelve or more main species of shark, of which only two have been reported as being man-eaters. One is the *blue shark*, which reaches a length of about 12 feet, and the other is the *whale shark*, which ranges in length from 35 to 60 feet. The blue shark is found only in warm seas, while the whale shark is found in all seas. All sharks are potentially dangerous to the diver, and the cardinal rule is never to run from one.

Even when a diver retreats, he must face the shark as he swims away, with a *backward* movement of his fins.

More deadly to the diver is the *barracuda*, whose greatest weapon, aside from its jutting jaw with rows of sharp teeth, is its fantastic speed in the water. It can remove an arm with one bite! There are twenty or more species, from 3 to 10 feet long, but the only one the diver must fear is the *great barracuda*, which inhabits the West Indies and the waters off the coast of Florida. This fish is fascinated by bright shiny objects, so the diver must remove any equipment of this nature in order to protect himself.

The *moray eel* is another species of marine life that is deadly to a diver exploring the waters of the West Indies and Florida. The *green moray*, which can reach a length of 60 feet, prowls these waters. Another species of moray eel is found in the Atlantic Ocean near the New England coast. Some inhabit the waters off the southern coastal states and others are found in the Pacific Ocean. Eels nest in rocks and divers must be careful not to invade the nests. The Romans kept the moray eels as pets in ponds. At times they served a more practical purpose; unwanted slaves or those who were to be punished for offenses were fed to the eels.

Sting rays, which resemble giant bats, have long tails that are barbed for inflicting injury upon attackers. The *electric ray* can sting a diver with an electric current sufficient to put him in shock and cause drowning. Rays inhabit the West Indies and are also found off the coast of California.

The *octopus* has been the object of many sea stories, but it is not as deadly as its reputation. Its famous arms with the tentacles are 20 feet long. It has a beak which contains a venom that will paralyze its victim.

In the same family we have the *squid*. The squid is aggressive and will travel about, while the octopus does not move and will

13

not attack unless disturbed. The giant squid grows up to 50 feet in length and has ten arms, two of which are much longer than the others. The tentacles are giant suction cups on the inner side of the arms. It will grasp an object with its tentacles and pull the object, either fish or diver, toward its deadly beak.

The larger species of marine life are not the only danger to the underwater explorer. The smaller varieties can be equally dangerous. All species of marine life have protective mechanisms that help guard them from harm, either from humans or other species of marine life that hunt them. The sea is never overpopulated, as all species of marine life feed upon their brothers of the sea. Their protective mechanisms enable them to survive if possible, and most species will not attack unless they are wounded, or, in the case of sharks and barracuda, if there is blood in the area.

Of the small species, the *Portuguese man-of-war*, the *jellyfish*, the *sea urchin*, and the *scorpion fish* are the most dangerous. The Portuguese man-of-war lives in colonies and like the octopus puts forth tentacles, which may range up to 40 feet. Each little organism has only a few tentacles, but when they are grouped together you can see the danger of a diver being stung violently. Hospitalization is necessary after such stings! The sea urchin uses its spines, which break off in the skin of the diver, as defense. These spines will have to be removed immediately, or infection will result. *Sea snakes* and *scorpion fish* use poisons, as do their counterparts on land. The well-known *lobster* can be a menace because of its claws.

Last but not least is the *killer whale* of the *dolphin* family, famous in legend and mythology. This small whale, which only grows to a length of 25 feet, has been known to attack large fish and also seals. It is small in comparison to its big brothers, but its teeth are deadly and all divers must beware of it.

2

The Old Art of Diving

FROM the days of the ancient Greeks man has been diving. He has continually sought ways to prolong the time he can spend under water. He has also spent time seeking ways to dive into the deeper depths of the ocean.

In ancient times most diving was done for purposes of earning a living or for military purposes. Sponge diving and pearl diving have been carried on for centuries.

Written records provide accounts of some very ancient diving exploits. Most of these were connected with naval warfare. For example, Xerxes is said to have used combat divers. Alexander the Great used divers to destroy the boom defenses of Tyre about 333 B.C., and Aristotle wrote that Alexander himself descended in some sort of a diving bell. Several ancient accounts indicate that some crude means were used of supplying the diver with air.

Interest in diving increased after 1500 A.D., and many different

15

Even though the younger generation is quickly taking to water sports and diving, it is important that the beginner learn from an experienced diver.

rigs were designed. In 1511, a book originally written by Vegetius in 375 A.D. was reprinted, and its drawing of the diving hood described became the first design for a diving dress to be found in a printed book. In 1680, Borelli proposed an outfit that would probably have been the first self-contained diving apparatus — if it had been built and could have been used, which is unlikely.

Although little of the equipment designed before 1800 was very practical, underwater accomplishments were surprising in many ways. Diving bells and crude diving helmets were used for work on wrecks as deep as 60 feet, and reasonably practical air pumps were developed before the end of the 1700s.

The forces that act upon a diver under water are explained by the science of physics, which deals with the behavior of all kinds of matter. The effects of these forces on the body are explained by physiology, which is concerned with the body's functions and its response to various conditions. We will look at this in Chapter 4. Both of these sciences have developed within fairly recent times. Archimedes explained *buoyancy* many centuries ago, but little was known about pressure and its effects until Robert Boyle did his experiments in the 1600s. Practically nothing was known about the composition of air or even the existence and importance of oxygen until Priestley's work in the late 1700s. Understanding of the body's vital functions of breathing and the circulation of blood developed even more slowly. It is not surprising that progress in diving was at a standstill for thousands of years and that men of high intelligence designed rigs that would not have worked.

The first real progress in diving came about mainly through increased knowledge of physics and advancement in invention and manufacturing. For example, divers could not go beyond very shallow depths until workable air pumps and hoses became available. This did not happen until around 1800, when steam engines began to be used extensively. Some of the most serious diving problems did not arise until progress made it possible for man to be exposed to high pressures. *Decompression sickness* was unheard of until caissons were put into use after 1840. In the years that followed, scores of men were killed or maimed by decompression sickness before the great French physiologist, Paul Bert, experimented with animals and applied existing knowledge to explain this condition, in the 1870s. Improvement in decompression methods and the beginnings of *recompression treatment* followed his work, but needless deaths and suffering continued until investigators like Haldane put the matter on a firmer basis in the early years of our own century. Much the same sequence of events also took place with *nitrogen narcosis, oxygen poisoning*, and other diving problems.

Today's divers have no cause to look down on their ancestors in diving for their ignorance. The average person today, although he

17

A Navy deep-sea diver helps a mate onto stage during diving training. The Navy's Diving School is located on the Anacostia River, Washington, D.C.

U. S. Navy

enjoys all the benefits of science, knows little more about physics and physiology than they did. In diving, we still face many problems that are unsolved because of our own lack of knowledge. The least every diver can do is to learn the essentials of what is known in these sciences as they apply to diving.

The advent of compressors to supply air started the development of diving as we think of it today. With the ability to maintain an air pocket against greater and greater pressures for longer and longer times came the problems of working under pressure. As each problem was encountered, its solution was sought through the combined efforts of the scientists and the men willing to try again. The most important development of this period was the "closed dress" invented by Augustus Siebe in 1830.

Not much is actually known about the beginnings of diving in the United States Navy. Although good work evidently was done at

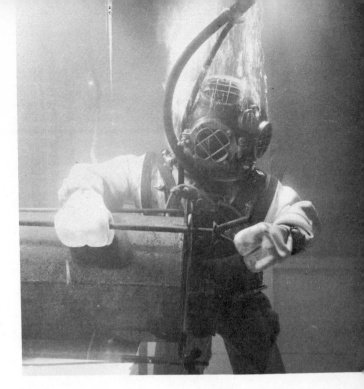

Deep-sea divers must learn how to patch up sunken ships, pump the water out of them, and attach pontoons to lift the wreck to the surface. This diver is connecting a pontoon.

U. S. Navy

shallow depths in the early days, very little was accomplished in deep diving. Largely as a result of the efforts of Chief Gunner George D. Stillson, an active development program was started in 1912 to check the practicability of a stage method of decompression and to improve the standard Navy diving gear to permit deeper dives. Extensive tests were conducted in diving tanks ashore and later on the U.S.S. *Walke* in Long Island Sound. The value of the work was evident in the salvage operations on the submarine U.S.S. *F-4* off Honolulu in 1915. On that job, divers descended to 304 feet — a depth which is probably a record for useful diving in the standard rig with air as the breathing medium.

The need for further development of diving was strongly emphasized by a tragic accident in the mid-twenties. On September 25, 1925, the U.S.S. *S-51* was rammed by the steamship *City of Rome* and sank in 132 feet of water off Block Island. The *S-51* was finally raised on July 5, 1926, and towed to U. S. Naval Shipyard at Portsmouth, New Hampshire. The many difficulties encountered were made more serious by the fact that so few divers had been trained to work at such a depth.

There was concern over the possibility that rescue and salvage operations would be needed in much deeper water. Divers could not retain their mental clarity and effectiveness when breathing air at great depths, so some other breathing medium was needed. Experiments on animals, later verified by studies with human subjects, clearly showed that helium-oxygen mixtures offered great advantages over air for deep dives. (Air is mainly a nitrogen-oxygen mixture.) The Experimental Diving Unit was established to work out practical means and safety standards, and has functioned accordingly up to the present.

The U. S. Naval School, Deep Sea Divers was originally established prior to World War I, but was closed and the instructors used for wartime diving work. It was re-established in 1926–27 at the Washington Navy Yard. This location was chosen with the view that its proximity to the Experimental Diving Unit would permit expeditious application of approved experimental findings to the standard training curriculum. The diving school facilities include two pressure tanks, capable of withstanding 350 pounds working pressure and 525 pounds test pressure. Each is directly connected to a recompression chamber. The two open tanks are also used for training. There is a large steel diving barge in the Anacostia River adjacent to the school, and two diving boats used for training and emergency work. A boat for deep-sea diving, another converted for salvage use, and a third converted to diving and rescue, complete the school surface fleet.

The tragic submarine disaster of 1925 spurred not only further progress in diving but also developments in submarine escape and rescue methods. The submarine escape mechanism (Momsen

Salvage worker getting ready to go down. The deep-sea equipment used here employs air pumped from a compressor on board ship rather than scuba tank carried on the diver's back.

U. S. Navy

Lung) was one result. Another was the McCann submarine rescue chamber. Two years of experimentation which had been devoted to the technique of helium-oxygen diving and to the so-called Mc-Cann chamber paid dividends in 1939. On May 23 of that year the U.S.S. *Squalus*, a submarine of the newest type, sank in 243 feet of water off the Isle of Shoals in the North Atlantic. On May 24 the U.S.S. *Falcon*, veteran of the *S-51* rescue job, arrived with the rescue chamber. During the next twelve hours the rescue chamber made four descents, and all thirty-three survivors were safely brought aboard the *Falcon*. The rescue chamber was then attached to the after hatch of the *Squalus*, but the sad news was reported that all was flooded and there were no signs of life.

Salvage work began immediately on the *Squalus*. This resulted in the first field application of helium-oxygen diving. On September 13, 1939, the *Squalus* was towed into port, following months of heroic salvage work. Had air alone been available as a breath-

One-piece underwater exposure suits worn by Navy underwater demolition teams.

ing medium, it is doubtful that the demanding job could have been accomplished.

With the expansion of the Navy to include ships specifically designed for ship salvage work and the requirements of diving under wartime conditions, it was necessary to increase the facilities for the training of divers. The Naval Training School (Salvage) was established on a permanent basis in September, 1942, to provide for the increased need for divers. During 1946 the school was transferred from Pier 88, New York City, to Bayonne, New Jersey. This school was authorized to train and designate salvage divers. In the summer of 1957, the faculty moved the school to Washington. In addition to the Deep Sea Divers, there are diving activities within the fleet and at various naval shipyards, which are authorized to train and designate divers second class.

During and after World War II, the Experimental Diving Unit continued the improvement of helium-oxygen equipment and techniques. Dives as deep as 561 feet were made, using helium-oxygen gear in the wet pressure tanks. Divers today are doing more kinds of underwater work and doing it at greater depths, for longer times, and with far greater safety than would have been thought possible a hundred years ago. The progress of the next century may be even more impressive. Certainly, the Navy's efforts to increase the scope and safety of diving will continue.

The Navy employs several different types of diving equipment, depending upon the circumstances and the job to be done. The two main categories are *surface-supplied* and *self-contained.*

All of the types in the first group are supplied with air or some other suitable breathing medium through a hose from the surface. They are used mainly where the diver's work is confined to a rather small area and where stability rather than mobility is important. The fact that air supply duration is not limited is a definite advantage of this type of equipment.

A photo diver in full dress with Cousteau Gagnon Aqualung, face mask, and swim fins or flippers.

U. S. Navy

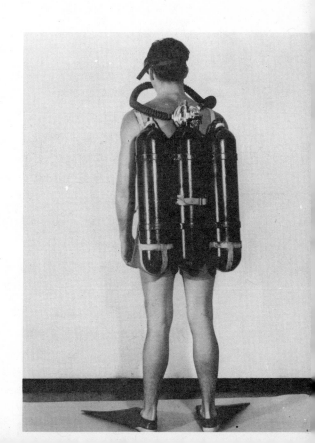

The surface-supplied deep-sea-diving outfit consists of a helmet and watertight dress, weighted belt and shoes, supply hose and control valve, non-return valve, and a spring-loaded exhaust valve.

Helium-oxygen equipment is basically the same as the standard deep-sea outfit. The helmet is modified by the installation of a means of conserving the helium-oxygen mixture by recirculating it through a carbon dioxide absorbent.

The essential part of the lightweight diving outfit is a full-face mask that is supplied with air from the surface through a hose. A non-return valve and control valve are mounted on the right side of the mask, and an exhaust valve is provided on the left side. This mask can be used alone, if desired, allowing the diver almost as much freedom, within limits, as self-contained equipment. A light, flexible dress is provided for use with the mask when desired.

The term "self-contained" indicates that the diver carries his breathing medium with him in cylinders and can thus be independent of surface connections. Three types of self-contained underwater breathing apparatus (scuba) are in present use. Each type may include more than one make or model of unit, but the basic principles and characteristics are essentially the same.

Most developments in diving stemmed from the need to accomplish some specific kind of underwater work. As diving itself progressed, and as new tools and techniques were developed, more and more types of underwater activity became possible. Today, men dive for purposes ranging from warfare to pure sport.

Raising sunken ships or repairing damaged ones is one of the most important applications of diving in the Navy today. Present-day ship salvage work is a specialized job that can put to use most types of diving equipment and almost every special skill a diver can have. It can require use of air pressure tools, use of explosives, underwater cutting and welding, and other techniques, as well as the specific know-how of salvage work itself. The underwater

Deep-sea diver resting after job well done. The 56-pound rubberized canvas diving suit is supplemented by the 85-pound belt, 54-pound helmet, and diving shoes weighing 25 pounds a pair.

U. S. Navy

phases of ship salvage usually consist of repairing damaged ships, raising sunken ships, refloating grounded ships, and clearing harbors. The Navy has several types of salvage ships, most of which are equipped with divers and several types of diving equipment. These ships are capable of performing all varieties of ship salvage work, from simple underwater repairs to major refloating operations.

Each submarine squadron has a submarine rescue ship (ASR) fully equipped and ready to aid a submarine in distress. Each carries a submarine rescue chamber, and its crew is prepared to perform all kinds of diving. ASRs are the only ships in the Navy whose crews are equipped for helium-oxygen diving.

Navy divers are not usually utilized in construction work, but much work is accomplished by divers in building tunnels, bridges, caissons, and occasionally wharves and piers.

Although history indicates that divers were used in war in very early times, tactical diving in military operations is comparatively new in modern warfare. It was developed into a very potent weapon of both offense and defense during World War II.

Many of the characteristic operations of underwater demolition teams can be conducted without diving equipment, but the ability to approach enemy beaches without surfacing is highly advantageous. Divers may prove to be the only effective defense against individual attacks on ships. Direct interception of swimmers and underwater hand-to-hand combat are not very probable, but periodic ship-to-bottom search may be essential.

Diving for pearls on a commercial basis has apparently been going on since before 4500 B.C., and it still continues. Sponges and several kinds of seafood are also harvested commercially by divers in many places.

Especially since the development of highly practical self-contained diving equipment, many scientists have been doing their research work under water. Those who study the mysteries of the ocean itself, the oceanographers, were among the first to do so. Marine biologists are now able to study underwater life in its natural surroundings. Many geologists are now diving, spurred by the clues that rocks and sediments can provide concerning the possibility of oil deposits beneath. Even archaeologists are going under water. Finding an ancient wreck sometimes gives them more information about a bygone civilization than digging in dry-land ruins. A few handy spelologists (cave exploring enthusiasts) have discovered that diving makes the exploration of caves even more interesting than it was before. Advancements in underwater photography and television have increased the scope of diving for many scientific purposes.

One of the most remarkable developments in the history of diving has taken place in the relatively short time since World War II — the popularity of sport diving, which continues to grow in almost all parts of the world. Although many sport divers confine themselves to skin diving without breathing apparatus, many thousands of them have acquired self-contained gear and are able to make dives that, just a few years ago, only professional divers could consider. Civilian interest has not only promoted the development of new kinds of diving equipment, but it provides a large reservoir of experienced divers who may be able to contribute to defense in the event of war.

Work closely related to diving is primarily that which requires the use of compressed air and in which working personnel are exposed to pressure. There are also types of underwater work which, although related to diving, are not performed under pressure.

A *diving bell* is a heavily constructed box or cylinder, open at the bottom and large enough to permit at least one man to work in it. When the bell is submerged, compressed air supplied from the surface is used to keep the water out and to provide ventilation. The submarine rescue chamber, which is standard equipment on all U. S. Navy submarine rescue ships, is in some ways like a diving bell, but with the difference that the men who descend in it are kept at normal atmospheric pressure. The chamber has a large reinforced vent hose to the surface which keeps the interior at atmospheric (surface) pressure. It is also supplied with electric power and communication cables, a compressed air supply hose, and a steel lifting cable. A steel downhaul cable is either brought to the surface by a buoy released from the disabled submarine, or attached to the submarine's hatch by a diver. The upper end of this cable is attached to an air-driven winch inside the chamber. By means of this, and by using its ballast tanks, the chamber is able to descend and ascend under its own control.

3

Diving in the Navy

THE salvage vessel mainly used in the Navy is the ASR type of ship, which is especially constructed to salvage sunken, stranded, or damaged ships. The commanding officer and most of his other officers are divers and salvage experts, and a large crew of divers and all their necessary equipment is carried. Other vessels, mainly the ATF (seagoing tug) type, and shore stations such as naval repair facilities also engage in salvage and have divers in their crews.

The ASR-type vessel is specially outfitted to rescue the crews of sunken submarines and later to assist in their salvage, if necessary. The submarine rescue chamber, or diving bell, is lowered to the stricken submarine from the ship, and then functions as a sort of underwater elevator to bring the trapped men to the surface. Divers are required to locate the submarine and attach the cable on which the rescue chamber is raised and lowered. Navy divers are

Members of the UDT are trained to conduct unconventional operations, such as preparing beaches for amphibious landings, blowing up enemy barricades, harbors, piers — and collecting intelligence about enemy ships and installations.

used for a great many miscellaneous jobs, such as small repairs that can be made without putting the ship in dry dock; searching for torpedoes, mines, and a thousand and one other things that can get lost on the bottom; and working on piers and other stationary objects under water.

Second class divers, the lowest of the various Navy classes, perform routine underwater jobs, usually at fairly shallow depths, under the supervision of master or first class divers. They are trained at several stations having large numbers of divers, or at the Deep Sea Divers.

Scuba divers are a special class of diver, who have been trained only in the use of scuba equipment and do not use deep-sea diving gear. They are trained only to fill particular specialized jobs, usually at the Underwater Swimmers' School at Key West, Florida. Many of the Navy's frogmen underwater demolition team members are also scuba divers. All divers of other classes are also required to know the use of scuba equipment.

First class divers are the journeymen of the diving field. They are qualified to perform any diving jobs, including salvage work, either in deep-sea diving dress or using scuba. They can dive to about 500 feet using helium and oxygen for breathing, 300 feet using compressed air, and about 130 feet in scuba gear. Each has received at least 26 weeks of concentrated training at the Deep Sea Divers, which is the only place in the Navy where first class diver training is given.

Master divers, as their title states, are the masters in their field. Each is a chief petty officer who has served at least a year on both salvage and submarine rescue vessels and has been especially recommended by his commanding officer. He then attends a special course at the Deep Sea Divers, appears before a special selection board of master divers and diving officers, and finally is designated as a master diver by the Chief of Naval Personnel. He is then qualified to supervise all diving operations and to supervise the mixing of the special mixtures of helium and oxygen used at depths below 300 feet. At the present time, there are jobs for only some 64 master divers out of over 600,000 men in the Navy.

Navy hospital corpsmen are also trained as divers. Although their main purpose is medical assistance, they must know the conditions under which their patients work; so they receive the same training as a first class diver, and then an additional two weeks of training in physics and medicine above that already given all divers.

Many enlisted divers are promoted to officer status and continue

Navy frogmen leave the submerged submarine *Sealion* through the forward escape trunk during exercises off St. Thomas, Virgin Islands. The frogmen belong to the Navy's UDT units — Underwater Demolition Team.

diving as officers. Most of the commanding officers of submarine rescue and salvage vessels, as well as the Officer in Charge and staff officers of the Deep Sea Divers, are former enlisted men, whose years of practical experience as divers make them ideal supervisors. Practically all other officers assigned to duty on diving vessels are sent through courses at the Deep Sea Divers.

Just as enlisted hospital corpsmen are trained as divers, so are the medical officers assigned to ships or stations where diving is done. These medical officers are given special courses at the diving school, including actual diving. Due to the similarity in the medical problems involved, submarine medical officers are first trained as diving officers, and then go to submarine school.

Members of the Navy's UDT No. 13, detachment of the U.S.S. *Burton Island,* take a cooling dip in icy waters off the Prince of Wales Strait during arctic expedition some years ago. The frogmen were carried to blast icebreaker out of pressure ridges with explosives if she should get stuck.

There is no way, at present, that a young man may enlist in the Navy with a guarantee of being trained as a diver. After he enlists, he must advance to at least the third pay grade and be recommended for training in one of the specialties from which divers are taken, such as shipfitter, boatswain's mate, and so forth. He can then apply for training as diver second class. When he has advanced another pay grade to third class petty officer (second class for hospital corpsmen) he is eligible for first class diver training.

After a man has volunteered for diving training, he is given a physical examination and various special tests to determine if he is physically and psychologically adapted for this type of training. He is given a color blindness test, pressure- and oxygen-tolerance tests, an actual dive, and finally an interview with a diving officer.

If he fails any of these or shows signs of fear in closed places, he is not suitable for training as a diver. A good estimate is that 50 percent of the men in the Navy could pass these tests. Of those actually applying, the number passing is much higher.

It takes more than just being in excellent physical condition to become a diver — muscles are no good without brains to direct them. Men applying should be at least average in general intelligence, and should have a high school education. The training courses include physics and other subjects requiring use of mathematics. A man must also be well motivated — that is, he must have more than just a notion he would like to be a diver. He must want to be one strongly enough to be willing to work hard and study hard to become one.

The U. S. Naval School, Deep Sea Divers at the Navy Yard in

A Navy deep-sea diver attaches a retrieving line during salvage operations in 200 feet of water from the submarine rescue vessel U.S.S. *Petrel* off Nassau in the Bahamas.

U. S. Navy

Mike Freeman

Spear fishing is among the most popular underwater sports. But it takes experience and skill to handle the spear gun under water, and it must be handled with great care. It is as dangerous as a high-powered rifle.

Washington, D.C., is an interesting and unique facility. A large brick building houses both the school and the Experimental Diving Unit. The pressurized tanks used to simulate great depths of water are so heavy that they were put in place before the building was completed, and the remainder of the building constructed around them. Other facilities of the school include classrooms, offices, metal and carpentry shops, air compressors, mixing and storage facilities for helium and oxygen, a complete Medical Department, and a locker for scuba gear. A barge is permanently moored at the pier outside the school building to provide additional classroom space, facilities for practice diving in the river, and scale models of equipment.

At present, all officers of the diving school are former enlisted men who spent many years as divers. The instructors are all first

34

class or chief petty officers and first class or master divers, who were especially selected for this assignment and are also graduates of the Navy's Instructor School. The medical staff is composed exclusively of diving medical officers and diving hospital corpsmen. The other members of the staff do not have to be divers, but many are, and others frequently train and qualify as divers when they can be spared from their regular jobs.

As a beginner becomes more skillful at diving he moves from the tanks inside the building to the barge and the almost black waters of the Anacostia River. Finally, he reaches the most advanced phases of his training, which are conducted on three vessels equipped to give him practical experience as close as possible to what he will encounter when he graduates and reports aboard a ship of the fleet.

Navy divers are learning how to work under water, mainly for the purpose of salvaging ships. This student is seen bolting a flange on a barrel pontoon.

U. S. Navy

The *YF-336* is a converted cargo-carrying vessel which is used for the ship salvage project. On this project a class of divers is given the blueprints for a sunken ship (a small LCI landing ship is used). Then they dive to inspect for holes, etc., and plan how to raise it. After a week or more of putting on patches, constructing cofferdams, and various other tricks of the trade, they start pumping out some of the water and forcing out some with high-pressure air until their sunken ship is afloat again. In actual salvage jobs it would then be towed off to be repaired, but here they turn right around and sink it again so the next class can also practice raising it.

The *YDT-5* looks like a small tug, but actually was once a minesweeper. It takes divers down the river to where deeper water can be found, and there they practice underwater work at depths up to 100 feet. Diving with helium and oxygen, as well as air, can be conducted from this vessel.

The *YSD-39* is a seaplane wrecking derrick mounted on a flat-bottomed hull which can operate in as little as four feet of water. It is used for raising and lowering the school's submarine rescue chamber, which is identical to those found on the ARS submarine rescue vessels, and for a variety of smaller jobs, as well as actual salvage operations in the Washington area when needed.

Other craft include LCM and LCP amphibious assault boats converted for diving. Some projects include a week of scuba training in the river and a week of underwater demolition training. Quite frequently, the police or other agencies request that divers be furnished to search for lost or stolen items in the river. These opportunities are used for additional practical training, with students doing the work under the supervision of school instructors. If you ever want to get rid of anything so it can't be found again, don't do it where there are Navy divers!

The Experimental Diving Unit shares the building with the

Paul Tzimoulis

A more courageous way of fishing under water is to catch lobsters with your bare hands. This requires some pretty fine technique that is not learned overnight.

diving school, but its work is entirely different. Where the school teaches the methods that have already been proven safe and practical, the Experimental Diving Unit is constantly doing research on how to dive deeper and longer, with less time on the way up without getting the *bends,* from too rapid a return to the surface. Another important function is the testing of the many new types of diving equipment and accessories that are constantly being invented and put on the market.

A complete knowledge of salvage techniques is necessary for the Navy diver. The U. S. Navy salvagers are called upon to raise ships that sink in harbors and block traffic in and out of ports. The Navy had such a mission in Guam in 1962. A typhoon struck the island with winds of a velocity up to 170 m.p.h. Several ships sank in the harbor, and the Navy was detailed to raise seven of them.

One ship had been facing a concrete jetty, and the force of the impact had cracked the concrete for a distance of 40 feet. The bow of the ship was completely mangled. Acetylene torches had to be used to cut away the torn metal. Fortunately, the bulkheads of the ship were intact and extensive patching of the bow was not necessary. The Navy divers made several trips to the hull, which was sunk in approximately 45 feet of water, to determine the extent of damage to the hull. In all salvaging expeditions this is the first step. The second fact that must be determined is whether the bottom where the ship is sunk is solid. If there is any danger of the ship shifting, the divers could be killed. If the ship is lying at an angle, the first step is to right it to make it easy to raise. Huge floats are sometimes used for this purpose. The deflated rubber floats are attached to the ship's bow and stern by chains passed under the ship. At times the divers must make tunnels in order to pass these chains under the ship. This is very dangerous work and the chances of a diver being injured or cut are obvious. It is a slow, tedious process. The ship could easily move from its position, particularly if it is lying at an angle and not completely on its side.

Navy salvaging ships equipped with large cranes are sometimes employed to literally lift the sunken ship out of the water. The ships are equipped with *booms*, in Navy terminology, which are cranes. These are fastened to a chain which passes under the ship's stern, as are the chains fastened to the floats. The floats are inflated with air and they will raise the ship and put it in a vertical position. The booms do the same thing. When the ship is in a vertical position it is easier to work on and the extent of damage can be determined quickly and easily.

The next step, after righting of a ship by booms or floats of varying sizes and purposes, is to patch the holes in the ship. The

38

jagged metal must be cut away with torches so that danger of cuts is minimized and easy access to the interior of the ship is possible. The *tooker plate,* named for its inventor, is one of the patches commonly used to seal portholes and small holes in the ship. It is a circular patch that folds in half and has a metal shaft secured in its center. The folded half is inserted in the hole and pulled outward in open position. The pressure of the water within the ship pushes it outward, and a screw with a long vertical bar secures it to the outside of the ship, keeping the patch in place. Tooker plates can be used again and again in salvage work and this is their prime advantage. Other patches are handmade of wood by the Navy salvagers. Plywood is used extensively because of its light weight. The wooden patches are backed with a layer of foam rubber to ensure as tight a fit as posible, and they are secured to the ship with the same type of screws as the tooker plates.

When the ship has been patched to the point where it is as watertight as possible, the booms may be employed to lift it out of the water. When the ship reaches the surface, the pumping begins with large motor-driven pumps which have been inserted in the interior of the ship. Compressed air is sometimes used to pump water out of ships, depending, of course, on the salvaging job. The salvaging techniques used depend upon the depth of water in which the ship has sunk, the stability of the bottom, the damage to the hull, and many other factors.

If the bottom is unstable, a *coffer dam* is used to raise a ship. A coffer dam is really an additional hull built around that portion of the ship which extends above the water line. The water is pumped out after the dam has been completed, and the ship will rise. Coffin dams are generally only used in cases where ships have been sunk in very shallow depths, and where extensive patching is impossible because of severe damage to the ship.

4

Secrets of the Diving Science

THE main difference between the physical properties of water and air causes many pleasant and unpleasant experiences for a diver. Man does not have three-dimensional freedom in air, which is a gas, but the liquid characteristics of water give man more unrestricted freedom of movement. Water, because it is a liquid, is heavier than air, and the density (weight) of the water restricts the speed of movement of all living things that travel under water, as well as ships and other mechanical devices invented by man. There are differences in acoustics (sound) in water, and although sound travels much faster under water there is a great deal of distortion of sound and light, and therefore communication under water can be a problem to a diver.

Light rays bend and are refracted (dispersed in different directions) and the appearance of objects is altered in relation to size, color, and distance. This is called *distortion*. Even the operation of the lenses of the eyes is affected under water.

Navy divers training in the Bering Sea. Much of the information gathered by Navy divers throughout the world is made available to our oceanographers in their continuous effort to learn more about the ocean.

Water will absorb four times as much heat as air, and therefore a drain on the heat store of the body is another factor in underwater activity.

The effect in diving of the water's temperature must be given careful consideration. The comfortable temperature range for man in the air is from 60 to 80 degrees Fahrenheit. Higher or lower temperatures in air can be tolerated without any serious physical effects to man for a fairly long period. These deviations in temperature ranges are much more limited in water. The unprotected diver cannot long cope comfortably with temperatures below 70 degrees Fahrenheit. Below 60 degrees protective suits are required.

When water is too warm (80 degrees and up), activity will be limited as well. The degree of comfort and endurance in regard to these temperature ranges is a factor that depends upon the physical condition and age of the individual involved.

When considering temperatures in relation to water, one must think in terms of heat contained within a liquid element. Water is a far superior conductor of heat than air, and the amount of heat loss from the human body is greater in a liquid than in air. Because the heat capacity and conductivity of water are so great, the need for protection of the human body in water for extended periods of time is important.

Certain materials have greater *conductive capacities* (ability to carry or retain heat) than others. The human skin will give off heat rapidly in water. Therefore, a material must be used that will control this heat loss as much as possible. Natural rubber has a very low conductive capacity and is very widely used as a material in diving suit construction. Dry woolen underwear also has a low conductive capacity. The standard equipment for *dry suit diving* is usually composed of a ¼-inch wool underwear suit and a ⅜-inch rubber suit (standard thickness for U. S. Navy diving suits of this type). Diving suits of a greater thickness than ⅜ inch begin to present a problem of buoyancy. Suits that are too thin have a tendency to tear or rip. The underwear worn beneath the suit will lose its low conductive capacity when wet, and heat loss will result. There will also be changes in the buoyancy of the underwear as trapped air is replaced by water.

Perhaps the most important thing about water is the pressure it exerts or forces upon objects floating in it.

Matter is composed of molecules. In water, the molecules are packed closely together so that they form a liquid. The deeper the water is, the more closely packed molecules become. In air, which is a gas, molecules are spaced far apart. In the air which exists at sea level molecules are much more closely packed together than they are at the level of a high mountain peak. Airplane pilots suffer from altitude sickness at great heights because of the thinness of the air in the atmosphere. The packing of these molecules results in matter being changed from a gas to a liquid and then to a solid. This process can also be reversed. Temperature (heat) is responsible for these changes. Because water is a liquid and much heavier than air, the actual weight of the water at lower depths can exert tremendous pressure. When molecules are spaced far apart there is less pressure (weight) involved than when they are compressed together and held in greater attraction. Therefore, one can easily see that pressures caused by great depths of water would be greater than pressures exerted by air at sea level. Although air is

Navy divers in the arctic surfacing to warm their faces in the sunshine. The **suits** protect the entire body area **except** a small portion of the face.

U. S. Navy

a gaseous mixture it still has some density, and the pressure at sea level is 14.7 pounds per square inch. Our bodies are not crushed by this pressure because the body tends to *equalize* the pressure by absorbing the gases found in the air. Air is composed of 21 percent oxygen, 78 percent nitrogen, and a small amount of carbon dioxide and other gases. The gases that we breathe are called *metabolically active* gases. They are light gases by weight and are very active. We breathe in oxygen and give off carbon dioxide. Nitrogen is a metabolically *inert* (inactive) gas, but our bodies still absorb this gas. Nitrogen's effect on the body in great depths can be fatal, as we will see in the next chapter.

The depth measurements of water are computed in two basic ways. One *atmosphere* is equal to 33 feet of distance down into the water. The pressure measurement for the *first atmosphere* is computed by adding 14.7 pounds per square inch to the pressure measurement per foot of depth in the first atmosphere of water. In other words, the weight of the air at sea level must be added to the weight of the first 33 feet of water in order to give an accurate measurement of pressure at any further depth.

The deeper we travel under water the greater the pressure becomes, as the molecules are squeezed more closely together. It is usually possible to dive in the first atmosphere without diving equipment and without any pressure problems. Beyond this depth, pressure becomes important in diving as a factor affecting the functions of the human body. Skin divers safely dive in this range without compressed air tanks, with face masks only.

In the next six atmospheres the need for diving suits and compressed air tanks (scuba equipment) becomes urgent for dives of any duration. Up to six atmospheres, or 198 feet, is the safe range for scuba equipment. The extreme pressures at lower depths make diving with scuba equipment impractical and unsafe, because the mixtures of gases (oxygen, helium, carbon dioxide) fed from the diving equipment must be controlled carefully to safeguard the life of the diver. Deep-sea diving equipment is usually used at these depths, and the air supply is fed to the diver from the surface through his hose. A helium-oxygen mixture is usually used at depths of more than 200 feet.

In scuba diving the tanks (cylinders) used are filled with compressed air, not compressed oxygen. The greater the depth of the dive the more compressed air the diver will require, and it is important in diving to consider the amount of air each cylinder will deliver at different depth levels. When a diver plans a dive of 200 feet, it is necessary to know how long the air will last at this depth.

The greater the pressure and depth, the faster the air will be consumed by the diver. The scientist Boyle stated that "if the temperature is kept constant, volume will vary inversely with the absolute pressure." This is a definition of the principle of squeezing of molecules. As an example, a balloon will shrink in the water and swell when heated. Another scientist, Charles, discovered the second important principle that has been applied to diving. He states, "If pressure is held constant, volume will vary directly with the absolute temperature." This principle becomes important in diving when divers may have to rise too quickly to the surface because of an emergency. Pressure decreases on the way up and too much air absorbed too quickly in the lungs expands them to the point where they might easily burst. The air molecules become more widely spaced apart as the pressure of deep depths ceases to "squeeze" the lungs. Many deaths have occurred in diving because of fast returns from great depths.

When a diver descends into the water he must be sure that there is always enough air in his lungs to *equalize* the surrounding pressures of the water he is traveling in. The surrounding pressures, *ambient pressures*, are constantly bearing down all over the body; the air absorbed by the body must equal that of the ambient pressures. Otherwise the end result may be death. If an air hose broke, the diver would be literally "squeezed" to death.

A large part of the human body is composed of water, and air will dissolve in water. Air is a light active gas and oxygen will exert one-fifth of the total pressure of the air at sea level. Nitrogen, carbon dioxide, and other gases exert the remaining pressures in the air mixture. The body does not absorb more than 5 percent of the total 21 percent of oxygen in the air. The amount of oxygen the body can absorb safely is one of the most important factors to be considered in diving, as well as the amounts of nitrogen and carbon dioxide. If the body is completely denied any air at great depths or if the amount is not kept constant with the pressures in the water, the deadly "squeeze" will occur. If pressure decreases too quickly and too much air is absorbed, the lungs will burst.

Objects float or sink in water because of their weight, not their size. A large piece of cork will float on the surface of the water, whereas a coin will sink immediately to the bottom. Size is not the most important factor to be considered in regard to objects that float upon the water. In spite of its tremendous size, a large ocean liner will not sink. The ability of an object to float in water is termed its buoyancy.

The density of an object is determined by its mass (or weight) per unit of volume. The coin we mentioned has a higher density than the cork. A cork will float on the water's surface, but an ocean liner does not. A part of the ship's hull rests *under* the water. The amount of hull that rests under water signifies its *displacement* in water.

If the ship is an object with high density, why doesn't it sink? The answer to this question was solved by the Greek scientist Archimedes. He stated that a body placed in a liquid is buoyed upward by a force equal to the weight of the water it displaces. A body that is less dense than water, such as a cork, will float, and

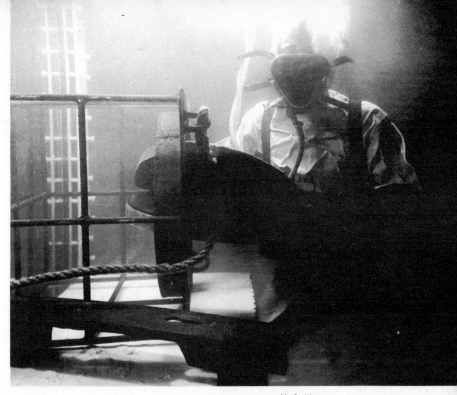

Student diver in standard Navy shallow water diving outfit
preparing to fit a tooker patch on a mock-up of a porthole.

one that has a density greater than water will sink. Cork is filled
with large air spaces that lessen its weight. Metal has much fewer
air spaces and is heavier. But water will support the ship by push-
ing it upward with a force equal to the weight of that portion of
the ship which is under water.

The human body, being composed to a great extent of water,
has a density almost equal to water. A body's air spaces tend to
lessen its density as well. That is the reason man can move freely
in the water and ascend or descend as he chooses. As the pressure
of the air on land is equalized by the air pressure that exists in his
body, the pressure of the water is equalized by the pressure of the
water and the air in his body. The ability of man to equalize pres-

sure without compressed air equipment only exists primarily in the first atmosphere, and in order for him to stay in the water for extended periods of time, he must use diving equipment. The scuba equipment, which consists of mask, tank or tanks of compressed air, and diving suit, enables man to function in depths beyond the first atmosphere.

Slight changes in buoyancy, man's ability to remain in one level under water without either sinking or rising to the surface, may occur as the air tanks empty, but these changes are not significant enough to endanger the diver. The diver can maintain his buoyancy at lower depths only for the reason that the air in his body equals the pressure of the water outside. If he receives too little air from the tanks he will sink, and too much air will propel him quickly to the surface. In the case of too little air received by the diver, the pressure of the water would push him down and compress his tissues in the process.

Light travels through water at only three fourths the speed of that which it achieves in air. When light rays go through water, they bend because of the barrier created by the water. Light traveling upward will bend in the same manner as it passes into the air. The speed of light is slowed down by the water, and the rays cannot travel as quickly as they do in air. This change of light rays as they travel from water to air and air to water results in the distortion of objects under water. The diver will find that objects in the water seem closer and larger than they actually are. The lenses of the eyes, if exposed directly to the water, lose their normal functioning characteristics, and further distortion results. This distortion is corrected by the use of the face mask, which interposes a layer of air between the eyes and the water and corrects this malfunctioning of the lens. The blue color of the sky is created by the *refraction* of light on particles of dust in the atmosphere. In the

48

same manner light is refracted by the particles in water. Images become blurred in water because of this.

Humidity can fog the mask of a diver easily under water and cut down his vision. This fogging happens because of the condensation of moisture from the breath. There are anti-fog compounds to correct this condition. In underwater photography this condition can interfere with the ability of the photographer to obtain clear pictures; it is necessary to use moisture control compounds to control the condensation on the face of the camera. Without such compounds pictures would be blurred.

Light cannot penetrate very deeply in water, so that it is impossible to photograph objects beyond 100 feet without some means of artificial light. Surface storms and lack of sunlight directly overhead can reduce the penetration of light rays considerably. Color photography is quite difficult under water. Because light is refracted in air by much the same principle as in water, the red colors are lost by absorption in the first few feet of water. The oranges follow, then the yellows at around 30 feet, and at 60 feet only the blues are left.

One may think of the ocean as a great soundless depth, but this is not so. The water is filled with the sounds of the living creatures that inhabit it. The movements of waves and boats fill the depths with sound. In complete contrast to light rays, sound travels under water *more* quickly than it does in the air; approximately three times as fast. One can hear sounds over great distances quite clearly. Vocal communication under water is limited, however, because of the difference in the viscosity of water in comparison to air. Sound waves travel from the air in the face mask to the water, and much of the sound energy is lost in this transition. Compressed air being exhaled by the diver creates difficulty in communicating sounds from the face mask. Conversation is therefore limited between divers under water at any great distance. In emergencies it is common practice for a diver to tap his tank sharply in order to gain the attention of other divers. Sounds created in this manner will travel great distances in water.

Because of the ability of sound to travel so quickly in water, it is difficult to localize sounds under water. This is particularly true of the motor sounds of boats traveling on the surface, and a diver must take extreme care when surfacing not to hit his head on one of them. Distortion of sound can be an extremely important problem to the diver.

Archimedes' principle of buoyancy has been applied to the use of carbon dioxide as a safety device in diving. Carbon dioxide is a light, active gas and tends to rise to the surface of the water quickly. Divers may use small cylinders containing carbon dioxide as a propulsion device to speed them up to the surface in case of emergency. These cylinders work much like a rocket, sending the diver upward when the carbon dioxide stream is directed downward.

The rate of movement of objects through the water is also determined by its *viscosity*. The water resists movement of objects because of the great weight of water forcing itself upon the object from all directions. Archimedes' principle can also illustrate the force of viscosity (resistance), which is "that property of a body in virtue of which, when flow occurs inside it, forces arise in such a direction as to oppose the flow." The pressure of the water will force itself upward against any object resting in the water, as seen in the principle of buoyancy. By the same principle, though not the same force, any object moving through the water will meet a force of equal resistance to the force which is being exerted by the object in the water.

The total surface area of an object can be an important fact in overcoming the viscosity of the water. A ship like the *Mayflower* is a far cry from the long, streamlined hulls of today, which are designed particularly to overcome the forces of resistance of the water. If there is no force of propulsion such as wind, a motor, or swimming, a ship, a fish, or a diver is unable to move in the water. Therefore, it is easily seen that a diver will not be able to swim very fast at great depths, where the viscosity and pressures are greater than at the surface.

The wind is force enough to overcome the resistance of the water at the surface, and it will propel a sailboat through the water, but a submarine or diver must find stronger means of propulsion in order to travel at any speed under the surface of the water. The submarine is equipped with an engine, but the diver has only the motion of his arms and legs to propel him through the water. The average rate of swimming speed achieved with scuba equipment is .8 to .9 mile per hour.

5

Safety Under Water

THE physical dangers of underwater swimming are explained by the science of *underwater physiology*, which is the study of the physical effects on the human body of water. For purposes of this science we may look at the human body as a mass of solid tissues with several air spaces such as the sinuses, the lungs and airways, air pockets in the stomach and intestines, and spaces connected with the ears. In all these spaces where air travels through the body, there is extreme danger of injury in diving.

Air does not travel completely and freely in all of these air spaces. Often a membrane separates the air traveling through the body from air spaces inside the body, such as in the lungs and the outer chest wall. When air travels into the body and pushes against these membranes, the air on the other side is pushed together or compressed. There is a point where compression ceases because of a rigid wall, such as the bony rib structure surrounding the lungs. A diver in a deep-sea helmet has the rigid wall of the helmet, and air flows between the helmet and his head. If his air hose breaks, the pressure will immediately force him down deeper in the water. The air supply to equalize the surrounding pressure of the water has been cut, and the diver will be literally squeezed to death by the pressure of the water which flows inside of his helmet.

The Eustachian tube is connected from the nose to the ear. A sufficient amount of air normally travels through this passage. If it does not, equalization in diving cannot take place, because the pressure outside will not be balanced by the pressure inside of the ear; and the eardrums will burst if the difference in pressure is great enough. The same pressure situation can take place in the sinuses and in the lungs. Hemorrhages or ruptures occur when any of these air spaces fail to equalize the pressure of the water outside. There will be extreme bleeding from the mouth and ears in such cases. Damage to the lungs is one of the most serious injuries that can develop under water. The lungs always contain at least a quart or so of air that is not exhaled. This air cannot be compressed any further. Without an additional source of air the lungs become squeezed against the chest wall.

As stated in *The New Science of Skin and Scuba Diving*,* instructors in the Navy submarine escape training tank must cope with the problem of lung squeeze. Air tanks are not used here, and the diver must hold his breath for a distance of 100 feet in order to retain sufficient air in his lungs. If air is lost on the way down only the compressed air in the lungs is left, and the blood vessels start to rupture. Any air lost coming up will result in the same condition.

* Conference for National Cooperation in Aquatics (Association Press, New York, March, 1962).

Underwater photography is becoming more and more popular. This Navy diver uses an Aquaflex camera, taking pictures for the television series *Navy Log*.

Squeeze also occurs in the masks and suits of divers as air is compressed under pressure at great depths. Exhaling in the mask or the release of more air into the suit will ease this condition.

The compression of air causes its density or weight to increase as the molecules become more closely packed together. Difficulty in breathing at depths results from this weight. It is four times harder to breathe in water as it is in air, because compressed air is four times as heavy as the air we breathe in the atmosphere. An extreme amount of heavy work can be almost impossible in diving because of this breathing difficulty.

When a diver begins his ascent to the surface from a deep dive, he can experience the most dangerous of all injuries in diving — the *air embolism*. Air embolisms have occurred in dives in an ordinary swimming pool with breathing equipment, so depth is not always a factor, but there is more danger in dives at great depths. As the pressure of the water decreases and the diver rises, the air molecules in his lungs spread apart. This is similar to the example given of the balloon. When the balloon is heated it will swell. The same process occurs in the lungs. If too much air is taken into the lungs without proper exhalation (breathing out), they can burst or an embolism may be formed. The dangerous point for the formation of an embolism exists in the upper levels of the water, such as the last 10 feet. At this level the lungs are filled with a maximum of expanded air, and if the breath is held for an instant, air is forced into the bloodstream and air bubbles are formed which block the flow of blood to the tissues. The tissues are starved for life-giving oxygen and die within a matter of minutes. Extreme injury or death is the result of an air embolism. Therefore divers are kept in the upper levels of the water in the decompression process for longer periods of time than any other in the ascent to prevent this from happening. When air embolisms occur, the patient is immediately put in a *recompression chamber,* where pressures are forced on his body of approximately the same amount that existed when the embolism occurred. The air in his lungs is immediately compressed, the air bubbles decrease in size, and circulation of the blood starts again. If accidents of this nature take place where a recompression chamber is not available for immediate use, the results are usually swift and fatal to the human body. When a diver using scuba equipment begins his return to the surface, the cardinal rule to remember is to exhale constantly. Divers are always taught never to hold their breath as they ascend.

At the Deep Sea Divers in Washington, D.C., a decompression tank is used to train the divers how to ascend and descend properly under varying pressure conditions. Pressures up to the degree found in 250 feet of water are forced upon the divers in this tank. The effects of the pressure on the diver are noted and he is taught how to ascend and descend properly from such pressures. On a fifteen-minute dive of 190 feet, the diver ascends the first 170 feet in approximately 2.8 minutes. His ascent in the remaining 20 feet of water includes two *stops*. He remains for four minutes at the 20-foot depth and seven minutes at 10 feet, before he is allowed to surface.

As stated before, the longest stop is the last one. The diver's lungs are completely filled with air and the danger of air embolism in this depth of water is greater after a deep dive. The diver is kept in the water a sufficient length of time during ascent to ensure his safety before he is allowed to surface. The longer a diver stays on the bottom at great depths, the greater the period of time needed for recompression. In very deep-sea diving with extended periods of time at the bottom, one or two hours, or more, may be required before a diver is allowed to surface.

Man is limited by the false atmosphere he carries with him under water in the form of compressed air tanks in scuba equipment. Compressed air has an important bearing on the time he can spend under water, the amount of oxygen he can consume, the effects that carbon dioxide can have on his body, and the deadly effect of nitrogen absorption by his body at lower depths and pressure. Extreme exertion under water will cause the diver to consume more oxygen than he normally would on land, and the possibility that he might run out of air is increased. Other injuries can result from a lack of oxygen for any reason. In the normal breathing process our bodies burn the oxygen in the air and give off carbon dioxide. The body has built-in mechanisms for automatic control of this process. A false atmosphere throws off the normal functioning of these mechanisms, and the body is not

Professional photographers must use a light meter to get the proper lens setting. Light rays are distorted under water, and light does not penetrate very deeply.

always alerted that too much oxygen or carbon dioxide is being absorbed. A danger signal may not come until serious and painful injuries occur.

Under conditions of a lack of oxygen supply, the diver will eventually lose consciousness and drown. When the tissues of the body do not receive enough oxygen they will die. *Anoxia* is the name of the condition that occurs when the diver is starved for oxygen.

Two types of equipment are used in scuba diving. One is an open-circuit type of breathing equipment, in which air is delivered directly from the tanks through a tube to the mask. Carbon dioxide is exhaled directly into the water through an outlet valve or another tube. Breathing takes place in the same fashion as it does on land. This is the equipment most commonly used by divers. The diver is limited in the amount of time he can spend under water by the amount of air in the tanks he carries.

The second type of breathing equipment is called *closed-circuit oxygen rebreathing equipment*. Long periods of time can be spent under water with this type of equipment, because a *carbon dioxide filter absorbent* removes this gas from the breathing equipment as the diver exhales and recirculates the oxygen supply through the breathing tubes. The unfortunate drawback of this equipment is that the body, because of the lack of proper functioning of the breathing mechanisms, may not be warned if too much carbon dioxide is being absorbed in the system. This may happen if the carbon dioxide filter becomes wet. Carbon dioxide poisoning results. The diver may overexert himself working under water and use up more oxygen than he knows with this type of equipment. The carbon dioxide mechanisms will drop equally and the nitrogen in the air mixture will satisfy his breathing urge. He will not realize that he has used up all of his oxygen, and anoxia and drowning will result. Closed-circuit equipment is never used at depths greater than 25 feet.

We have 21 percent oxygen in the air we breathe on land, although our bodies can only absorb 5 percent of this total amount. The minimum oxygen percentage of air to which we can be exposed is 17 percent, before dizziness, a lack of coordination, and other symptoms of oxygen starvation begin. If the body receives less than 10 percent of oxygen at any time for a long period of time, death will result. The only warning is a feeling of dizziness. Dangerous brain damage can be another result of anoxia.

Excessive carbon dioxide buildup (carbon dioxide poisoning) is not fatal, but the diver can lose consciousness and drown. The symptoms are the same as those in anoxia.

Foreign gases which may poison compressed air tanks will cause poisoning of the body as well. Carbon monoxide flowing from an engine pumping compressed air in a tank can poison the tank. The diver would be completely unaware that his tank was poisoned and would not realize the dangerous situation that he was in.

Dalton's law teaches us that gases exert pressure proportional to the amount they make up of the total volume of the mixture. Compressed gases force much more pressure on the body in breathing mixtures than gases do in the air at sea level on land. Nitrogen makes up 79 percent of the air mixture. When it is compressed under water it will exert tremendous pressure on the body, particularly at depths of 150 feet and below. When the body ab-

A deep-sea diver using an oxygen-arc torch for underwater welding and cutting.

U. S. Navy

sorbs too much nitrogen under pressure the sensation of dizziness results. Nitrogen has a strange effect upon the human body. Divers reaching a depth of 200 feet begin to suffer from *euphoria,* a happy feeling of not caring what happens. This is followed by a complete lack of concentration; divers find it impossible to read pressure instruments or even their watches. This state is called *nitrogen narcosis.*

Dentists use nitrous oxide or "laughing gas" when filling cavities, and if you have ever had a tooth filled in this manner, you have experienced this sensation. A diver could cut his air hose, remove his air tanks, or do other foolish things under these circumstances without fully realizing what he was doing. The famous writer and undersea diver Jacques Costeau, author of *The Silent World,* described this state as "rapture of the depths."

Helium, however, is a gas which does not have the anesthetic effects of nitrogen. It is used in dives beyond 200 feet to avoid nitrogen narcosis. Dives of 561 feet (pressure tank) and 600 feet (open sea) have been made successfully by the use of a helium-oxygen mixture. Deeper dives have been made possible by the use of helium-oxygen mixtures, but hours must be spent in decompression from such great depths and extended dives are limited because of the time factors. Scuba equipment cannot be used for deep dives because of the limited air supply of the tanks and the necessity of a constant supply of gas mixtures in larger amounts to equalize the pressures of the water.

There is another injury that can occur from nitrogen. Nitrogen narcosis is cured by simply ascending, but the deadly nitrogen *bends* occur by a process called *supersaturation.* As we explained, gases expand as the temperature rises and pressure on the human body decreases. What happens when nitrogen starts to expand in the body as the diver ascends from a deep dive? We have seen that air forms air bubbles in the bloodstream and that air embolisms result. Oxygen is absorbed by the body too quickly, to result in supersaturation, and the pressure that it exerts upon our body is not as great as that of nitrogen. Over three-fourths of the air mixture is made up of nitrogen and the pressure it forces on the body is proportional to its percentage in the mixture. *The New Science of Skin and Scuba Diving* gives a simple example of supersaturation. It is illustrated by what happens when an ordinary carbonated soft drink is opened. When the bottle is capped, the gas and the liquid are held together by pressure. The bottle is opened and the pressure drops quickly. The gas mixes with the liquid, very quickly, and reaches a saturation point (maximum point of mixing with the liquid) where the pressure of the liquid is greater than the air, and the mixture starts to bubble or "boil." The same process takes place in the human body, when the nitrogen reaches a point of absorption in the human tissues and bloodstream where they can sustain no more, and nitrogen bubbles start boiling in the blood. Pain and convulsions occur when this happens, for the nitrogen blocks the flow of oxygen to the tissues. The bends occur when a diver ascends from great depths too quickly. Decompression is used once again to prevent the tissues from reaching a saturation point as the diver ascends and to give the body time to exhale this excess amount of nitrogen through the blood and lungs, as it normally does on land. Stops at various pressure depths are used to give the diver time to get rid of the nitrogen. The Navy has computed tables that show the appropriate time that the diver should spend at these levels.

The bends can be fatal if recompression does not take place quickly enough. If a diver is brought up too quickly, he is rushed to a decompression chamber at once and pressures are forced on his body to relieve this condition.

It is possible to make deep dives for short periods of time without danger of decompression sickness, either from the bends or air embolisms in the upper levels. The rate of ascent must be carefully planned in order to avoid the bends. The rate of ascent for dives of this nature is 60 feet per minute. If these standards are not carefully followed, decompression will not take place in a safe manner and serious injury can result.

The choice of diving equipment and its condition should be carefully planned and checked before a diver considers entering the water. Rebreathing devices cannot be used beyond a depth of 25 feet because of the effect that pressure has upon oxygen. Oxygen under pressures found beyond 25 feet will turn partially into a liquid. The lungs will be literally "burned" by the liquid oxygen and oxygen poisoning will result.

6

Equipment for the Sports Diver

DIVING equipment designs have been formulated since the sixteenth century, but it was not until 1825 that any workable self-contained equipment was designed, when William James designed a primitive scuba diving outfit. It consisted of a leather helmet with a window, a short diving suit with elastic arm-holes and waist, and an iron "air tank" in the form of a belt carrying 450 pounds of pressure per square inch. The standard tank today carries pressure of 2,265 pounds pressure per square inch. Four hundred fifty pounds at that time was a tremendously high pressure for a tank to carry.

As we know, compression of air means nothing more than squeezing the molecules together until they are so tightly packed that they have reached the ultimate point of compression. If air is compressed beyond this point, the tanks will explode. The amount of compressed air a tank will hold is of course proportional to its size.

Open-circuit scuba breathing apparatus has either a *single stage regulator* or a *double stage regulator*. A regulator consists of an air valve or valves which automatically allows air to travel through the breathing tube to the diver upon demand, and cuts off the air to the diver when demand for air ceases. The amount of air that a diver can receive will vary depending upon the pressure level in his tank. A two-stage regulator controls the amount of air fed to the diver and also regulates the pressure level in the tank, making sure that a sufficient reserve of pressure is built up to keep the diver supplied with enough air as the air is used up and the pressure in the tanks is lowered.

Diver with camera alongside sunken sub. Taking pictures of the sub may help surface salvage experts to determine how sub is damaged and what kind of rescue technique should be used.

U. S. Navy

Scuba diving has its disadvantages in that dives beyond 130 feet require decompression and limited air supply is a great factor. A tank that will give 40 minutes of air on the surface will only give the diver 14 minutes of air at 100 feet. Lack of communication with the surface is another aspect of scuba diving, making it impractical and unsafe. In case of accidents the diver cannot communicate with anyone on the surface unless he wears a life line, which can become entangled with underwater objects and which limits the distance he can travel. The deep-sea diver's helmet affords great protection but the scuba diver has only his mask to protect him from rocks and other sharp objects in the water.

The regulators attached to the air cylinder and breathing tubes are a very important part of the diver's equipment. There are three fundamental types. The first is the double hose. The mouthpiece, which is held between the teeth, is connected to two breathing hoses. One is for the purpose of inhalation and the other for the purpose of exhalation. The hoses are connected to the regulator, which controls the flow of air to the diver, and the exhaust valve, for getting rid of the exhaled carbon dioxide. The second type is the single hose, which is attached to the cylinders. The exhaust is placed on one side of a full mask, which covers the entire face. In the third type the single hose is attached to the mouthpiece and regulator, which form one single unit. The exhaust valve is attached to the mouthpiece. The proper functioning of the regulator is imperative to the diver's safety. A wide choice of regulators and breathing equipment is available. The choice is a matter of personal preference and the practicality of each different type of equipment for the diving job involved.

Aside from the breathing regulator a new device has been invented that will warn the diver when his air supply in the tanks is low, by means of slowing down the air supply so that the diver has difficulty in breathing, or by a sound device that is triggered when the air has dwindled to a certain pressure in the tanks.

One of the primary safety features of open-circuit diving equipment is the exhalation of carbon dioxide directly into the water. Non-return valves control any "backing up" that might occur in the breathing hose, which in the case of double hose equipment could cause carbon dioxide poisoning. There is no danger of oxygen poisoning with this type of equipment, either, because the air is not recirculated through the breathing equipment, as is the case in closed-circuit equipment, and the diver does not reuse the same air. With open-circuit equipment the diver must surface when his air supply is low.

All compressed air tanks that are used commercially are checked carefully according to the standards set by government agencies. All commercial tanks are registered by serial number with the Bureau of Mines. The Interstate Commerce Commission requires that the cylinders be stamped with a mark that notes the pressure capacity of the tanks, and that they be tested every five years to see that there are no leaks and that the tanks are in good operating condition. Such regulations protect all divers from purchasing imperfect tanks. Tanks should be checked in filling to see that contamination or poisoning has not occurred. Oil vapors and carbon monoxide from motors in the area will contaminate the tanks easily. As we know, poisoning can result from such contamination and death can be the result.

Flippers are used by the diver to achieve faster speeds of swimming in the water. The human foot was not designed for this purpose. The legendary mermaid has her tail, but man must rely on his flippers. Flippers extend the length of the human foot and adapt it for better use in swimming. The type that is closed at the heel is the safest, because of danger from rocks and other sharp objects.

Snorkels are breathing tubes that can only be used on the surface of the water. They are air tubes that fit in the mouth and connect with the air above the surface. These are extensively used in hobby diving. If the snorkel is attached to the face mask, it must be cleared of water after a dive. One does not have to lift the head in breathing while using a snorkel. With a snorkel a diver can see under water while swimming on the surface. In ancient times divers would use reeds in order to camouflage themselves from the enemy by remaining just under the surface of the water and breathing through them in a manner similar to that used by the hobbyist with the modern snorkel.

Navy divers are trained for many different tasks. One includes the salvage of sunken subs and rescue of the stranded crew if possible. This diver is seen approaching a submarine resting on the bottom of the sea.

U. S. Navy

The snorkel can be used effectively to look for divers or other objects in the water. The unlimited supply of air enables the diver to travel and see under the surface of the water for extended periods of time.

Two basic suits are used in diving. In scuba diving the *wet suit* of *neoprene* is used extensively. Neoprene is a coal tar material, which looks and feels like foam rubber. It is not watertight, and allows a small amount of water to pass through it and form a lining between the suit and the skin. The thin water lining is warmed by the temperature of the body and keeps the diver warm at depths where the water is cold or under any circumstances where he may find himself in abnormally cold water. Tears in the suit do not affect the diver's buoyancy or endanger the protective ability of the suit.

The *dry suit* consists of a rubber or plastic outer suit and a suit of dry underwear underneath. Since air is the insulator in a suit of this nature, there is the possibility that the diver may suffer from "air squeeze," as stated in *The New Science of Skin and Scuba Diving*, at great depths.

The air keeps the body warm. If the suit rips or tears, water will enter and soak the underwear, making it heavier, as the air is displaced by the water. Dry suits are used in very deep diving because of the high heat conductivity of air. The diver needs all the warmth and protection he can get at these depths, and the wet suit is not practical. All deep-sea diving suits are dry suits made of vulcanized heavy rubber. The deep-sea diver has a constant supply of air from the surface, and this is another reason why a dry suit is more practical for deep dives. More air pressure is also required for equalization at greater depths, and the wet suit is not adequate for this purpose. In all dry suits the danger of exposure to the water is a serious problem, because of buoyancy and the temperature of the water. A dry suit must cover the entire body of the diver. Wet suits in deep scuba diving must also cover the entire body, but for less deep dives where the water is warm a partial suit can be used.

A diver must carry a great amount of equipment with him in the water. It would be almost impossible for a man to carry all this equipment on land for an extended period of time because of its weight, but water, because of its buoyancy, carries part of this load for the diver. But heavy equipment can load a diver down and cause overexertion in the water, which is dangerous. The equipment can become entangled in underwater plants, seaweed, etc., and it could be fatal for a breathing hose to be torn or entangled. Extreme care should be given to the amount and weight of equipment a diver plans to carry under water with him.

A harness is used to attach the air cylinders to the body. The buckles should have a catch that operates easily, in case of emergency.

Some human bodies are more naturally buoyant than others. For this reason, the *weighted belt* that is used by scuba divers varies in total weight, depending upon the individual wearing it. All weighted belts should have clasps that open easily.

The necessity for a diver to shed his equipment easily during an emergency makes efficient equipment an important factor.

A great variety of masks are available for diving. The choice depends on the diving task involved and the equipment used. In full-face mask equipment, the mask covers the full face and the diver breathes normally through his nose. The regulator is attached to the mask. Fogging caused by the condensation of the breath from air to water can occur with this type of mask and the face will be covered with drops of water. A little water is allowed inside of the mask to clear up this condition, or anti-fog compounds can be used to prevent it. If water enters a mask accidentally, it is purged out by the use of a button attached to the regulator or a valve inserted in the mask. The exhaust breathing hose is used to purge water out of the exhaust tube and out of the mask if full-face mask equipment is used. The diver will lower the left side of his body, press on the right side of his mask near the regulator, and insert his fingers under the mask on the left side to allow a little water to enter. The water will then travel through his exhaust tube into the water. The mask will once more be filled with air and he will be able to breathe normally again. This technique and other methods of handling scuba equipment have been set forth in *The New Science of Skin and Scuba Diving* in great detail. A mask should be chosen with care. *Plastic lenses* will fog easily, so shatterproof glass is most widely used. Soft rubber should be chosen because a hard rubber mask will cut the skin under pressure. Goggles should not be used because of pressure on the eyes.

The advantages of scuba diving are many. Freedom of action in the water because of the self-contained equipment is one. Very heavy equipment is not necessary, nor is an air supply from the surface. Helpers who are required to aid deep-sea divers are not needed with this type of equipment. The deep-sea diver requires men to pump air, to help him in and out of his equipment, and to control the air hose and life line that are his only connections to the surface. All this labor is expensive. A boat must be hired to transport the deep-sea diver, with the necessary equipment on board to supply his need. Scuba equipment is much less expensive. A diving outfit of this type may cost two hundred dollars but a deep-sea diving outfit costs over a thousand dollars.

Deep-sea diving equipment is very heavy. The helmet alone weighs approximately 65 pounds. It is usually made of a brass alloy. The helmet is attached to the heavy rubber suit by screws. The diver's breathing apparatus is regulated by a system similar to that of the full-face mask in scuba diving. The regulator in his helmet is connected to the air hose which travels upward to the air supply on the surface, and the helmet has an exhaust for the carbon dioxide exhaled. There are glass portholes in the helmet from which he observes the undersea world. Aside from the heavy helmet he wears a weighted belt and heavy shoes weighted with lead, to aid him to descend to great depths and stay there. If a deep-sea diver has his hose cut, the only air supply he has, he will die. His heavy helmet and shoes will prevent him from escaping from his suit and if his life line is cut, the last link to the surface is gone. It is easy to see that deep-sea diving is dangerous. The scuba diver can shed his equipment easily. The deep-sea diver cannot take off his suit unaided.

Because of limited air supply scuba divers usually dive in depths of 30 to 200 feet. Deeper dives of short duration have been made up to 400 feet, a record in scuba diving. Beyond depths of 250 feet the deep-sea diver takes over. Air-helium mixtures are necessary and pressure factors make the deep-sea diving outfit the only practical diving equipment in these depths. The record for a dive of this nature in the open sea is 575 feet.

Deeper dives have been made with the aid of equipment that resembles diving bells, etc. Hans Keller, a famous diver, designed his own diving equipment. Built to hold two men, it rather resembles a diving bell, suspended from a chain. The gas he used was a mixture of his own invention. He achieved a record of 750 feet the first time he dived and recently made another dive of 1,000 feet, which is the record for a dive of this type. An accident occurred during this dive because of a gas leak in the diving apparatus and an Englishman, who was the second man in the bell, was killed because of the injuries he sustained by the lack of equalization of the pressure. Keller was injured, but thanks to his extremely fine physical condition the recompression chamber was able to save his life.

The bathyscaph is another man-made invention for plumbing

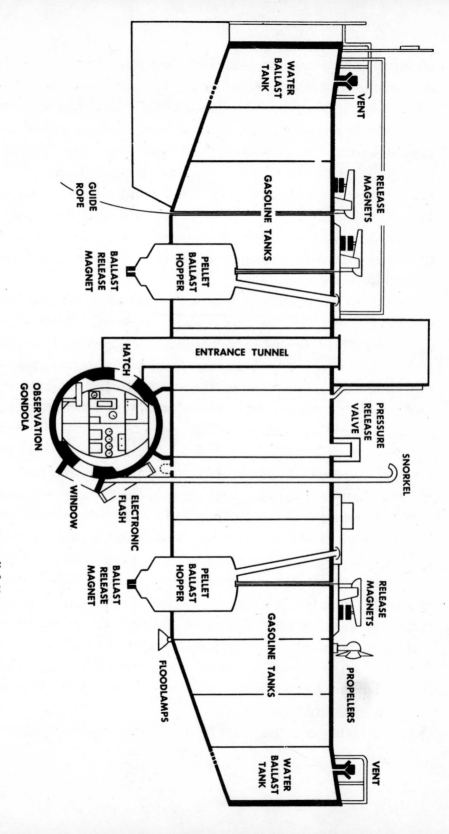

Schematic view of the Trieste. It was designed by Professor Auguste Piccard, one of the world's leading oceanographers. In January, 1960, the Trieste penetrated nearly seven miles down into the ocean. It was piloted by Lieutenant Don Walsh.

U. S. Navy

WATER BALLAST TANK

VENT

RELEASE MAGNETS

GASOLINE TANKS

GUIDE ROPE

BALLAST RELEASE MAGNET

PELLET BALLAST HOPPER

ENTRANCE TUNNEL

HATCH

OBSERVATION GONDOLA

PRESSURE RELEASE VALVE

SNORKEL

WINDOW

ELECTRONIC FLASH

BALLAST RELEASE MAGNET

PELLET BALLAST HOPPER

RELEASE MAGNETS

GASOLINE TANKS

PROPELLERS

FLOODLAMPS

WATER BALLAST TANK

VENT

the deep depths of the ocean. It is self-contained and lowers and raises itself by means of ballast and the ejection of gasoline from its float. The bathyscaph *Trieste* made a historic dive of 35,800 feet to the bottom of the world's deepest ocean trench, in the Mariana Islands near Guam in the Pacific Ocean, in 1960. Before the invention of the bathyscaph by Auguste Piccard, man was unable to explore such depths in the ocean. Further discoveries may enable him to travel freely in the ocean at great depths.

Water temperatures and climate in the area in which a dive is planned should determine the diver's choice of equipment. A fresh-water lake can become terribly cold at a depth of 25 feet or so, whereas the Gulf Stream extends its warm current to depths of a mile. Temperature variations are defined as *thermoclines.* Water generally becomes colder at lower depths, and the diver should gather information relating to temperature variations in the area in which he plans to dive. A general example of thermoclines is given in *The New Science of Skin and Scuba Diving.* In general, it is stated, if the air temperature is 85 degrees Fahrenheit, the temperature of the water at the surface will be 75 degrees. For the first 15 to 25 feet the temperature drop will average only a slight degree, and diving without suits is comfortable. Between 25 and 100 feet the temperature will drop another ten degrees, to 65 degrees. A suit is still not necessary in this temperature. From 100 to 300 feet the temperature drops another five degrees, and the use of a full wet suit with breathing equipment is necessary if a diver wishes to spend any time exploring at this depth. At 300 feet onward the temperature drops to 50 degrees and below, and the use of a dry suit is necessary for prevention of extensive heat loss from the body. Cramps can result at this depth if a dry suit is not used.

A diver must always check his equipment carefully before entering the water. Air cylinders must be transported very carefully.

If a cylinder of compressed air explodes, the force of the compressed air can propel it like a rocket through the air for a distance of at least three blocks! If a tank exploded, the clothes would literally be torn off any person standing nearby and more severe injuries could happen to anyone standing in the path of the cylinder.

The breathing equipment must be checked carefully as well. All breathing equipment should be washed with fresh water after each use to prevent salt-water corrosion and to keep dirt from forming in the regulator equipment. Corrosion and dirt will stop the breathing equipment from functioning correctly.

Having checked his equipment, the diver is now ready to descend into the water. A red flag with a white strip is generally used to signify the presence of a diving expedition. The Navy and Coast Guard use a solid red flag for this purpose. This is called a Baker flag. Divers can easily be hurt by the propellers of passing motorboats, and the sight of this flag warns the pilots that divers are in the area.

Aside from his diving suit and breathing equipment, the diver uses underwater tools for protection, for fishing, and for prying objects loose.

The spear is used for fishing. It is generally very sharp and must be handled carefully to avoid hurting other divers in the area. The three-prong spear is much like the triton used by the sea god, Neptune.

The *spear gun* can be compared to a high-powered rifle. It is just as dangerous, and the diver should be conscious of this at all times. Most spear guns are activated by a trigger, and the shaft is propelled by compressed gas, springs, or a slingshot type of propulsion.

Of the three the compressed gas type is the most dangerous. In some states the use of carbon-dioxide-powered spear guns is forbidden within a three-mile limit of the shore. Spear guns are very powerful and the spears travel at great speeds through the water. The danger of injuring other divers in crowded waters is quite easy with guns of this type. The spearing of fish with spear guns can be quite dangerous — divers have been towed to their deaths by powerful fish that have been speared! If the gun becomes entangled in the diver's suit and the lines from the spear gun become accidentally wrapped around him, he will not be able to free himself and will be towed until he hits some object in the water. The collision could be a fatal one.

Large fish travel swiftly through water and man cannot match this speed. Therefore, he must use his spear gun carefully with regard to the size of his quarry. Accidents can happen on land with carbon dioxide spear guns if they are left on the beach in the hot sun. The cylinders will explode, hurting bathers in the area. Extreme care must be given to any carbon dioxide spear gun.

The knife is another important underwater tool. It should have a cutting edge and an edge that will saw objects. Salt water will corrode knives and they will become dull. To overcome this, knives are coated with *silica gel,* a protective covering for metal.

A prying tool such as an iron or steel bar can be used under water. The edge does not have to be sharp, but it should be strong enough to aid in prying objects out of the sand or rocks. It should be fastened to the wrist. All tools should be either kept in sheaths or pointed away from the body at all times. The spears should always be pointed down as the diver ascends or descends.

It may be necessary for the diver to use his spear gun or knife for protection. He must view his attacker with caution. A wounded fish, such as a shark, will attack a diver immediately. Newly developed cartridge devices with gun shells have been developed to kill large fish. They are shot from spear guns. They enter the body of a fish and explode, killing the fish if they enter near the brain or vital organs. Extreme care must also be used with cartridges of this type.

The hobby diver generally will not run into large fish such as sharks and barracuda unless he dives in warm waters off the coast of Florida or in the waters of the Caribbean. In the Pacific Ocean near the coast of Australia sharks are very numerous. A diver should be aware of the type of underwater marine life that exists in the area in which he is diving, so that he will be able to protect himself adequately. The United States Coast Guard is one source of information for a diver. If there is a Coast Guard Station in the area in which he plans to dive, he should contact it for information regarding the tides and marine life in the area.

Some methods of protection are not achieved by tools. Experienced divers have been able to protect themselves from sharks by literally facing them! A shark does not have three-dimensional vision, as do human beings. This three-dimensional vision allows us to see objects in perspective, such as a man standing at the foot of a large mountain. Without three-dimensional lenses, our eyes would see the man and the mountain as objects of the same size. The shark does not have three-dimensional vision and, as objects already appear larger under water, the shark sees a man as a large mass in front of him. The shark cannot determine the depth of the man. He could be as long as a battleship. This gives the diver an advantage, and if he immediately moves toward the shark, in almost all cases the shark, if not wounded, will run. If a diver runs from a shark, the fish will almost always attack. A diver must not panic in such situations.

Another tool that is used by the diver for many purposes is the float. It can be used to carry his equipment when he is making an extended dive. An inner tube can be used. Floats are usually painted in bright colors. A brightly colored float will warn boat operators of the presence of a diver. Floats are sometimes used as rescue vehicles. Deflated tubes attached to cylinders of carbon dioxide are carried down to distressed divers and inflated, and then rise to the surface carrying the diver with them.

A diver should attach a line to his float and tie it around his body in order to keep the float with him as he travels under water. The loss of this float could mean the loss of valuable tools, such as spear guns, life preservers, etc.

As we have stated before, the diver has no contact with the surface in case of trouble. The presence of a float could mean the difference between life and death in diving. The deep-sea diver has a life line attached to his body which rises to the surface, and is held on board the ship from which he gets his air supply. If he is in trouble, he can tug on his life line and he will be pulled up promptly. Scuba and skin divers are not as fortunate, and therefore *diving in pairs is always preferable.* In an emergency, another diver can help the injured person immeasurably. If aid is impossible, at least the other diver can surface for help.

7

Underwater Treasure Hunts

THE oceans and the seas are vast treasure chests that await the hand of man to bring to the surface all the riches contained in the world beneath the water.

Man has been limited in his exploration of this world because of the inability of the human body to adjust itself to great pressures, and because of the lack of equipment to aid him in underwater exploration.

The sea has many species of marine life that have not been identified. The species at great depths are relatively unknown, and the sea monsters that have been reported for centuries may be different and larger species of the marine life already known, or new species completely unknown to man. In the future marine biologists will seek the treasures of the deep, name them, and place them in the great marine family in proper order and classification.

For the oceanographer there are great trenches to be explored,

U. S. Navy

The Aquabat under way. This model is a two-man, free-flooding submersible craft propelled by electric batteries. This equipment gives divers a considerable range and increases the duration of underwater search.

rock formations to be studied, and analyses of the mineral contents of these rocks to be made. The oceanographers are the underwater geologists. They will aid in the search for oil deposits which may exist in the ocean. Oil deposits have already been found in the Gulf of Mexico, and immense floating oil drills have been built to tap this wealth at the bottom of the ocean. The oceanographers have a world far more vast than that of the land to explore in future years.

The archaeologist will chart the history of the sea in a different sense than either the marine biologist or the oceanographer. Within his scope will fall the historic ships that have plunged to the bottom of the ocean depths from ancient times to the present. Billions of dollars of gold lie at the bottom of the ocean. There are treasures that equal those found in the ancient tombs of Egypt waiting for the archaeologist to salvage and study. Much will be learned about ancient cultures from the remains of these ships, and much valuable information will be gathered about the types of ships that were built during these ancient periods. Very little salvaging has been done relating to ships of the sixteenth and seventeenth centuries, and with the advent of better equipment and a broader knowledge of the locations of these wrecks, the archaeologist will be able to fill these gaps in history. He will seek not only ships but also the remains of cities that have been literally swept into the sea by earthquakes and tidal waves.

One of the seven wonders of the world is the Colossus of Rhodes, a statue of the god Apollo, one of the ancient Greek gods. The statue was made by Chares about 280 B.C., and it was 120 feet high. The remains of this statue, according to historical reports of its original location, lie somewhere in the waters of the harbor in the island of Rhodes. An archaeological expedition recently searched in this area for the statue, but was unable to locate a trace of it.

Within the Caribbean Sea there are several British and Spanish ships that hold vast stores of gold as a prize to the salvager who can claim the contents of these wrecks. These ships were the victims of storms, war, and privateers, such as the famous Edward Teach (Blackbeard) and Sir Henry Morgan, who made the Caribbean their stronghold and hunting grounds for unwary ships. Pirates flourished in the Caribbean from 1700 to around 1830. Stories of buried gold still lure salvagers and treasure hunters to the islands. Tortuga Island, off the coast of Haiti, was a famous pirate stronghold and search for buried treasure on this island goes on continuously.

A Navy UDT member leaving the water after ice reconnaissance swim. Knowledge of underwater ice conditions and phenomena help the Navy operate its subs under the polar cap.

From the time of Cortez's original expedition to the Aztec cities in Mexico, the Spanish galleons carried tons of gold and historic treasures of the Aztec culture back to the mother country. The Mayan Indian culture which flourished in Central America was another source of gold and treasure to the Spaniards. Some priceless relics of the Mayan culture were discovered in the waters of the Caribbean in 1908.

Several wrecks have been located off the coast of Florida. The Library of Congress in Washington, D.C., has several treasure maps showing the location of sunken ships and the reported amounts of treasure on board. It has been reported that approximately one thousand ships were sunk in the Florida-Caribbean area between 1500 and 1860! They were ships of all nations, and the treasure hunter has a vast storehouse in this area.

One of the most interesting treasure hunts in recent times was the raising of the Swedish ship *Vasa*.* The *Vasa* was a 1,400-ton armed galleon built for the Swedish Royal Navy in 1628. For unexplained reasons, the ship sank a mile out of the port of Stockholm, right after its launching. The full crew, some three hundred soldiers, and several women and children went down in approximately 110 feet of water. Some salvage attempts were made by an English engineer called Ian Bulmer shortly after the ship was sunk. Bulmer succeeded in completely righting the *Vasa*. Her masts were above the water, so horses were probably used. The next attempt took place in the 1660s by Hans Albrecht von Treileben, a Swedish army officer, and Andreas Peckell, a German salvage expert. They used a primitive type of diving bell, which was open at the bottom and had compressed air at the top level. At that time 53 of the *Vasa's* 64 guns were recovered. (This same type of bell was used in 1687 by Sir William Phipps when he recovered $1,500,000 from the Spanish galleon *Nuestra Señora*, which was wrecked on the Silver Bank reefs of the Caribbean.)

All further attempts were given up until a few years ago when a Swedish naval engineer by the name of Anders Franzen decided to search for the *Vasa* and raise her. After considerable research and with the use of echo-sounding equipment, Franzen discovered the large *Vasa* 300 feet outside of the harbor. For two years the ship was patched and repaired under water, and in May of 1961 she was brought to the surface. Gas floats and hydraulic jacks attached to pontoons on the surface helped raise the old ship. Chains from the jacks were passed under her hull to aid the salvage effort.

* *National Geographic Magazine*, January, 1962, Vol. 121, No. 1. Article by Anders Franzen, pp. 42-57.

U. S. Navy

The Navy is experimenting with different kinds of diving bells, rescue chambers, and small one- or two-man miniature submarines, such as this Aquabat.

The enemy of all salvagers and divers are the shipworms that ravage all wrecks and eat the hulls and all wooden parts that lie above the sand. In the Caribbean the coral worm feasts on wrecks, and in the colder climates the teredo worm destroys all wooden ships that have not been protected, even if they are afloat in a harbor. The teredo worm will only thrive in water that has a certain percentage of salt in it. The *Vasa* was spared the fate of many wrecks in other parts of the world; her hull was intact when she was brought up. A wood preservative was used to prevent the wood in the hull from disintegrating completely when it dried, or the hull would have fallen to pieces.

Treasure hunter and salvager Mike Freeman, owner of the American Water Sports Company in Washington, D.C., recently decided to form a treasure-hunting expedition to salvage the galleon *Genovase*, which was built in Italy and delivered to the Spanish in 1730. She was wrecked in October, 1730, off the island of Jamaica near the Pedro Bank, and the remains of the wreck lie in 35 feet of water. She was reported as having carried a large amount of gold bullion on board when she started the fatal voyage home to Spain. The gold is still there and Mike Freeman and a small group of adventurers formed an expedition in November, 1962, to hunt for it.

The bulk of the hull of the *Genovase*, which had been above the sand, had been eaten by the coral worms, and the divers really had to dig for their treasure. A type of dynamite was used to loosen the sand in the area so the divers could search more easily. They found part of the hull, the anchor, and several artifacts, including cannonballs, shot, and cannon, beautifully preserved because it had been packed for shipment to Spain in grease and canvas. They did not find the gold bullion, but Mike Freeman is planning another trip to continue the search. Sharks and barracuda were constant companions of the divers, and one of the party contracted coral poisoning and could not use his hands for three weeks.

Outside of the three-mile limit of any of the islands in the Caribbean, the treasure belongs to the salvager. If any is found within the three-mile limit, it is confiscated by the government. Florida is an exception, as she considers the wrecks historical sites and will confiscate only 25 percent of the treasure. The South American and Central American countries will confiscate treasure within the three-mile limit.

Man has been limited in his exploration of the sea by a lack of equipment in which to travel freely under water at great depths.

Navy frogmen also have special units called SEAL (sea, air, land). In addition to being trained in leaving and entering a submarine, they must be expert parachutists. They represent the most versatile soldier of today.

The submarine has given him some freedom but it has its depth limits. Man has not been able to spend time permanently in the sea, and such famous divers and explorers as Cousteau and Link are rapidly developing machines and equipment that will enable man literally to live under the water.

Inventor Edwin Link has developed a cylindrical diving capsule which will allow the diver some freedom within the chamber during decompression. The diver can eat and relax within the capsule during the decompression process. The capsule also operates as a base for underwater exploration. The diver can use equipment and leave the capsule for extended periods of time, until his air cylinders run out. He can then return to the capsule, which is supplied from the surface with a constant supply of an oxygen-helium mixture. He has also designed an underwater house, where the divers can live at depths of 200 feet. The Link capsule would act as an elevator to the surface.* A diver has been kept in this capsule at 200 feet for a record 24 hours and 15 minutes.

The discovery of oxygen-helium mixtures has given divers freedom from nitrogen narcosis, but the effects that helium may have on the body are unknown from a medical point of view, and such equipment as the capsule mentioned above will have to be tested extensively before the safety factors are determined completely.

Possibly the most interesting instrument developed for underwater exploration is the bathyscaph. The brainchild of Auguste Piccard, the bathyscaph is a valuable tool to man in the exploration of the ocean. Its only important limitation is its inability to travel great distances in the water. It has a range of only four miles, but it has carried man to the deepest trench in the ocean, a great triumph in man's endeavor to conquer the seas.

The bathyscaph works on the same principle as the balloon, which is filled with a gas lighter than air. By means of ballast and allowing some of the gas to escape, the balloon can descend to the earth. The bathyscaph is a large float filled with gasoline, which is lighter than water. As it descends, the pressure of the water compresses the gasoline and pulls it down. If the float hits a warm current of water as it descends it will stop, because the warm water will expand the gasoline in the float and it will stay at one point. Gasoline is poured out of the float to overcome this obstacle, and the float will continue its trip to the depths of the ocean. The lead weights, which are carried on board as ballast, are held together

* *National Geographic Magazine,* May, 1963, Vol. 123, No. 5. Article by Edwin Link, pp. 713-17; article by Lord Kilbracken, pp. 718-31.

in one mass by an electric current. When the bathyscaph is ready to rise from a dive, the current is turned off and the lead pellets are released through the bottom of the diving vessel. With the release of this weight the bathyscaph rises easily. The diving vessel has propellers to travel at the bottom of a dive, but underwater travel is limited. Great exploration of the ocean floor has not yet been possible, but other diving vessels in the future may be developed that will permit greater freedom at the bottom of the ocean floor.

One of the greatest inventions to aid the exploration of the underwater explorer has been the invention of *sonar*. Radar is used on land to identify objects and sonar is used in the waves. The system makes use of sound waves which bounce off objects in the water, giving pilots knowledge of them. Great icebergs travel down from the Arctic in the summer, their great mass hidden under the water. This can be fatal to ships, and due to fog and storms icebergs may sometimes not be sighted easily. Sonar warns the pilot of icebergs.

Recently, a sonar telephone was developed for means of underwater communication. The first sonar telephone was built at the United States Navy Electronics Laboratory at San Diego, California. It was used on the bathyscaph, and communication to the ocean floor in the Mariana Trench was maintained. The sonar telephone will give divers much greater safety as the ocean floor throughout the world is explored in the future.

The hobby diver, although limited by equipment and knowledge of salvaging, can still look for treasures near the shore. There are private schools throughout the country where he can learn the art of diving. Y.M.C.A.s throughout the country give courses in skin and scuba diving. They have set standards of age levels and medical standards and examinations for all young pupils interested in diving. Seventeen is the minimum age for scuba training, but skin divers range from twelve years old upward. A potential diver *at any age level must be trained by experienced experts.*

America's first undersea park was opened in 1960. It is called the Key Largo Coral Reef Preserve and it is situated off the coast of Florida. The actual name is the John Pennekamp Coral Reef State Park. It is approximately twenty-one miles long and four miles wide. Here the hobby diver can explore an area which contains all of the underwater delights of the ocean. All types of marine life frequent this park, and the diver can explore all species at his leisure. The underwater photographer can have a wonderful time taking photographs of the multicolored coral and the schools of fish. There are sharks, barracuda, and moray eels in the preserve, and extreme care must be taken not to disturb them, but the diver can explore with caution and pleasure.

The bulk of the ocean has yet to be explored, and the young diver can find many different fields relating to underwater exploration. Scientists, divers, salvagers, and underwater sportsmen are all contributing to the new science of oceanography. The world beneath the surface of the ocean presents a constant challenge to tomorrow's explorers. Someday they will conquer this "inner space" — a challenge equal in both magnitude and scope to the conquest of outer space.

Glossary

*The New Science of Skin and Scuba Diving**

"AB" — abbreviation for abalone.

ABSOLUTE PRESSURE — the addition of 14.7 pounds (one atmosphere) to indicated gauge pressure. True pressure.

ABSORBENT — a substance capable of taking something into itself. Rebreathers contain a chemical absorbent capable of removing CO_2 from expired breath.

ABYSMAL DEPTH — any vast depth. Prior to the invention of the bathysphere and other modern depth-probers, this designation was given to most depths over 300 fathoms.

AIR EMBOLISM — unvented pressure due to gas expansion forces air from sacs (*alveolae*) in the lungs into blood vessels. Resultant lack of blood causes tissue to die.

ALVEOLAR EXCHANGE — transposition of oxygen to the blood and removal of carbon dioxide in the alveolae of the lungs.

AMBIENT PRESSURE — pressure of water upon objects placed in it (surrounding pressure). It is usually expressed in terms of absolute pressure.

BACKWASH — water piled on shore by breaking waves sets up an outward current. Often called undertow or runout. This is an advantage when entering from the beach.

BAR — an offshore bank or shoal forming a ridge above the bottom.

BAROTRAUMA — injury due to effects of pressure.

BLUFF BANK — a bank usually located on the convex side of a river's curve which is subject to vertical plunges due to underwater erosion. Hazardous to divers and surface craft.

BORE — a single high wave moving upstream at the mouth of a river. Caused by incoming tide opposing river current. Knowing tide tables will prevent divers from being caught by this phenomenon. Synonym "Eagre."

BREAKWATER — a structure built to break the force of waves.

BREATHING AIR — commercially prepared or machine-compressed air free of contaminates that would be injurious to a diver operating under pressure.

BREATHING DEVICE — an apparatus that enables divers to breathe under water.

* Courtesy the Conference for National Cooperation in Aquatics. (Slightly revised to meet the requirements of this book.)

BUG — lobster.

BUDDY BREATHING — the sharing by two or more divers of the same tank. An emergency technique used when one person's air supply is exhausted.

BUOYANCY — the upward force exerted upon an immersed or floating body by a fluid. Neutral, positive, and negative: Neutral allows the diver to remain at a depth without effort; positive will cause the diver to rise toward the surface and requires effort to remain at depth; negative results in the diver's sinking toward the bottom, and can be dangerous if not controlled.

CALM — a wind of less than one knot or one mile per hour.

CHANNEL — the deeper part of a river, harbor, or strait.

CLOSED-CIRCUIT — oxygen rebreathing equipment.

COASTAL CURRENTS — movements of water that generally parallel the shore line. Such currents may be caused by tide or wind.

COMPRESSED AIR DEMAND TYPE UNIT — a breathing device using compressed air that is delivered to the diver through a regulator, as he demands it by inhalation.

CREST — maximum height of a wave.

CURRENT — a horizontal movement of water. Currents may be classified as *tidal* and *non-tidal*. Tidal currents are caused by forces of the sun and moon and are manifested in the general rise and fall occurring at regular intervals and accompanied by movement in bodies of water. Non-tidal currents include the permanent currents in the general circulatory systems of the sea, as well as temporary currents arising from weather conditions.

CYCLODIAL WAVES — inshore waves that are short and choppy and forceful when produced by strong winds.

CYLINDER — used in diving terminology to mean compressed breathing gas container.

DARK WATER — when visibility is reduced to a minimum by material in suspension or lack of natural light. Sport divers — stay out.

DECOMPRESSION — release from pressure or compression.

DENSITY — the weight of anything per unit of volume.

DIAPHRAGM — a dividing membrane or thin partition. The thin muscle separating the chest cavity from the abdominal cavity; also, the rubber or other material separating the demand chamber in a regulator from the surrounding water.

DISLOCATION WAVES — inaccurately called "tidal waves." Caused by underwater landslides, earthquakes, or volcanic eruptions.

DIURNAL — daily rise and fall of tide.

EAGRE — see *bore*.

EBB CURRENT — the movement of tidal current away from shore or down a tidal stream.

EBB TIDE — a tide that is flowing out or causing a lower water level.

EDDY — a circular movement of water, of comparatively limited area, formed on the side of a main current. May be created at points where the main stream passes projections or meets an opposite current.

EELGRASS — submerged marine plant (*Zostera marina*) with very long narrow leaves, abundant along the North Atlantic coast — called also *barnacle grass, grass wrack.*

EPICENTER — the focal point of great waves.

ESTUARY — where tide meets river current. A narrow arm of the sea meeting the mouth of a river.

EXHALE — to breathe out.

EXPIRATION — the act of breathing out or emitting air from the lungs.

FACE PLATE — glass or plastic window, so constructed as to provide air space between eyes and water and to permit both eyes to see in the same plane. The skirt makes contour contact with the face, preserving air space. Pressure may be equalized by breathing into the mask. Full-face plate — covers eyes, nose, and mouth. Regular covers eyes and nose only.

FETCH — "length of fetch" is the extent of water over which a wind blows and develops waves. The greater the distance the greater the possibility of large waves developing.

FLOTATION GEAR — any device employed to support the diver or to give additional emergency buoyancy.

FLOTSAM — wreckage of a ship or its cargo found floating on the sea.

FORCED WAVE — a wave generated and maintained by a continuous force.

FREE WAVE — a wave that continues to exist after the generating force has ceased to act.

FUNGUS — a group of simple plants that contain no chlorophyll and so must feed on living or dead plants or animals. (The parasitic fungi are most dangerous to man.)

GAUGE PRESSURE — the instrumental indication of change from normal atmospheric pressure level.

GROIN — a structure projecting from shore, designed to break the current and thereby check erosion and build out the shore by causing a deposit of new material.

GROUND SWELL — large, usually smooth-swelling waves.

HALF-TIDE LEVEL — also called mean tide level. A plane midway between mean high water and mean low water.

HEMORRHAGE — any discharge of blood from blood vessels.

HIGH WATER — the maximum height reached by a rising tide. The height may be due to periodic tidal forces alone or be augmented by weather conditions.

HOOKAH — a diving apparatus consisting of a demand regulator worn by the diver and hose connected to a compressed air supply at the surface. This is "free diving" but limited to one area by the hose length.

INHALE — the process of permitting air to enter the lungs.

INLET — a narrow strip of water running inland or between two islands.

INSPIRATION — the act of breathing in.

JETTY — a structure, as a pier, extended into a sea, lake, or river, to influence the current or tide in order to protect a harbor.

KELP — various large brown seaweeds (*Laminariaceae* and *Fucaceae*).

KNOT — velocity unit of one nautical mile (6,080.2 feet) per hour. Equivalent to 1.689 feet per second. To convert feet per second into knots, multiply by 0.592.

LAND BREEZE — a breeze from the direction of the land.

LANDWARD — in the direction of or being toward the land.

LEE — a sheltered place or side; that side of a ship that is farthest from the point from which the wind blows.

LEEWARD — pertaining to, or in direction of, the lee side. Opposed to *windward*.

LEEWARD TIDE — a tide running in the same direction in which the wind blows.

LEEWAY — drifting to the leeward caused by wind or tide.

LIGHT BREEZE — a wind of 4 to 6 knots.

LIMITING ORIFICE — a mouthlike tube opening or vent through which the passage of a liquid or gas may be restricted within specified limits determined by the diameter of the orifice and the pressure drop across the opening. In scuba equipment, the size of the orifice is such that the flow is reduced to less than the amount needed for respiration when the bottle pressure falls below a certain pressure, e.g., 300 pounds per square inch.

LONGSHORE CURRENTS — movements of water close to and parallel to the shore line.

MODERATE BREEZE — a wind of 11 to 16 knots (13 to 18 m.p.h.).

MODERATE GALE — a wind of 28 to 33 knots (32 to 38 m.p.h.).

MONSOON — the season of heavy rain in India and adjacent countries.

NARCOSIS — a state of stupor or arrested activity.

NAUSEA — any sickness of the stomach, with a desire to vomit.

NEAP TIDE — a "nipped tide" or "scanty" tide which occurs near the first and third quarters of the moon; is low because of the sun and moon pulling at right angles to each other.

NON-TIDAL CURRENT — current that is due to causes other than tidal forces. Classed as non-tidals are the Gulf Stream, the Japan, Labrador, and equatorial currents, which are part of general ocean circulation. Also classed in this category are river discharges and temporary currents set up by winds.

NURSING — see *buddy breathing*.

PARTIAL PRESSURE — the effect of a gas exerting its share of the total pressure in a given volume. Air, for example: Nitrogen 80 percent, Oxygen 20 percent at one atmos. 14.7 per square inch. Partial pressure: Nitrogen — 11.76 p.s.i.; Oxygen —2.94 p.s.i.

PHYSICS OF DIVING — the science of matter and motion as related to man's activities under water.

PHYSIOLOGY OF DIVING — the organic processes and phenomena dealing with life and functions of organs of human beings while in water environment.

QUICKSAND — sand that is partly held in suspension by water. Varying in depth, it easily yields to pressure of persons or objects. Resembles ordinary sand and occurs on flat shores and along rivers having shifting currents.

RECOMPRESSION — returning the diver to highest pressure endured (or greater if necessary) for the purpose of minimizing and eliminating the effects of decompression sickness, air embolism. This process is accomplished in a recompression chamber rather than in return to depths.

REEF — a ridge or chain of rocks, sand, or coral occurring in or causing shallow areas.

REGULATOR — an automatic device for maintaining or adjusting the flow of air equal to the ambient pressure of the water.

RESPIRATORY MINUTE VOLUME — the amount of air inhaled and exhaled per minute to maintain proper body function. This is variable, dependent on exertion and individual.

RIP CURRENT — a strong current of limited area flowing outward from the shore. It is usually visible as a band of agitated water in which the regular wave pattern is interrupted. This type of current is caused by the escape of water piled between shore and bar or reef by waves. The rush of escaping water is accentuated by its flow through a gap in the bar or reef. Such currents are dangerous to the uninitiated and the cause of many drownings at ocean beaches. However, when located by divers (skin and scuba) they are often used to facilitate entry to areas beyond the bar or reef.

RIPPLES — very small, gentle waves with little undulation.

RUBBER SUIT — partial or complete covering for the diver, primarily to insulate and preserve body heat. Classified as "wet" and "dry." Wet suits of foam neoprene (usually) permit a thin layer of water to contact diver's skin. Dry (rubber sheet) suits prevent contact with water but require the additional insulation afforded by cloth underclothing.

RUNOUT — rip current.

SANDBAR — a body of sand built up by action of waves or currents.

SCUBA — self-contained underwater breathing apparatus. Any free diving unit containing necessary elements to support life under water.

SEA ANCHOR — a drag thrown overside to keep a craft headed into the wind.

SEA BOTTOM SLIDE — a landslide under water, usually causing dislocation waves.

SEA BREEZE — a breeze blowing over land from the sea.

SEA NEWS — rip current.

SEA PUSSES — rip current.

SEAWARD — away from land toward the open sea.

SEAWAY — one of the sea traffic lanes or routes; a vessel's headway; an area where a moderate or rough sea is running.

SEICHES — geological term for dislocation waves.

SHOAL — a place where a sea, river, etc. is shallow because of bank or bar.

SINGLE HOSE UNIT — open-circuit scuba having a single high-pressure hose with first stage pressure reduction at the yoke (tank attachment), second or ambient reduction at the mouthpiece. The exhaust is at the mouthpiece.

SINUS SQUEEZE — damage of tissue lining or air sinuses in the head due to failure of pressure in sinus to equalize with ambient pressure. Pain in sinuses is the signal to stop descent; rise several feet (pain diminishes). Try again cautiously. If pain persists, don't dive.

SKIN DIVING — diving without the use of scuba or other deep-sea apparatus.

SLACK WATER — the state of a tidal current when its velocity is near zero, especially the moment when a reversing current changes direction and its velocity is zero. Occurs at high and low tide.

SNORKEL — a J-shaped tube, the short end of which is held in the mouth, the long end protruding above the surface, permitting breathing without raising the nose or mouth out of the water when swimming face down on the surface. Many types are available on the market, and experience will dictate which type is best for the individual.

SPEAR GUN — any device which propels a spear from a gunlike frame. Usually rubber, spring, or gas powered.

SPINDRIFT — sea spray, sometimes called *spoondrift*; the spray and water driven from the tops of waves by wind.

SPRING TIDES — the highest and the lowest course of tides occurring every new and full moon.

SPUME — frothy matter, foam, or scum usually collected at water line.

SQUALL — a gust of wind generally accompanied by rain or snow with nimbus clouds. Intense and of short duration.

STORM — winds of 56 to 65 knots (64 to 75 m.p.h.).

STRONG BREEZE — a wind of 22 to 27 knots (25 to 31 m.p.h.).

STRONG GALE — a wind of 41 to 47 knots (47 to 54 m.p.h.).

SURF — waves breaking upon a shore.

SURGE — a great rolling swell of water; a violent rising and falling.

SWELL — a large more or less smooth wave.

TANKS — a term also used to denote container of compressed gases.

THERMOCLINE — an abrupt change in temperature encountered at varying depths.

94

TIDAL WAVE — see *dislocation waves*.

TIDE — the periodic rise and fall of water level due to the gravitational attraction of the moon and sun acting on the earth's rotating surface.

TIDE RIP — waves and eddies in shoal water caused by tide.

TIDE WAVE — a long-period wave that has its origin in the tide-producing force and which displays itself in the rising and falling of the tide.

TOXIC — poisonous.

TROCHOIDAL WAVES — deep-water trains of waves that have great distance between crests with gentle slopes. They are the result of wind pressure, local or distant.

TROUGH — the hollow or low area between crests of waves.

TYPHOON — originates over low water and consists of winds rotating in counterclockwise motion at tremendous velocity (75 to 150 m.p.h.). Develops in a low-pressure center and is accompanied by high tides. Seldom travels in excess of 12 m.p.h. Diameter may range from 150 to 300 miles.

UNDERTOW — a seaward current near the bottom of a sloping beach. It is caused by the return, under the action of gravity, of the water carried up to the shore by waves or by onshore wind.

VALVE — a device that starts, stops, or regulates the flow of gas or air.

VOLUME — space measured by cubic units.

WAVE — an oscillatory movement in a body of water which results in an alternate rise and fall of the surface. Maximum height is called the crest or high-water phase; minimum height is called the trough or low-water phase. The period of a wave is the interval of time between the occurrence of successive crests at any given place. The length of a wave is the distance between two successive crests.

WAVE HEIGHT — the vertical distance from preceding trough to crest.

WHOLE GALE — wind of 48 to 55 knots (55 to 63 m.p.h.).

WINDWARD — the point or side from which the wind blows; toward the wind; in the direction from which the wind blows. Opposed to *leeward*.

YOKE — a device for attaching regulators to cylinders so as to make a leak-proof seal. Use no more than finger pressure to attach.

The Authors

Erik Bergaust has been observing and writing about aviation, rocket, and space flight development for the major part of his career. A native of Norway, he came to the United States in 1949 after a number of years' experience in aviation writing, editing and public relations work. He has been a project engineer for several aeronautical and missile engineering companies in this country and has also been the editor of several magazines.

William Foss spent most of his early life in Norway. When he returned to the United States he attended high school and soon after joined the Navy. Most of his time was spent aboard destroyers. Soon after his discharge he worked as a translator-researcher for the Central Intelligence Agency and in 1951 joined the staff of a weekly service newspaper in Washington, the *Navy Times*. He is now a writer for the U.S. Department of Commerce. The authors have written many books including *Helicopters in Action, Coast Guard in Action,* and *The Marine Corps in Action.*